ONE YEAR
–
AND BEYOND

Thomas K. Hofer

iUniverse, Inc.
New York Bloomington

ONE YEAR - AND BEYOND

iUniverse books may be ordered through booksellers or by contacting:

iUniverse
1663 Liberty Drive
Bloomington, IN 47403
www.iuniverse.com
1-800-Authors (1-800-288-4677)

ISBN: 978-1-4401-4847-7 (pbk)
ISBN: 978-1-4401-4848-4 (ebk)

Library of Congress Control Number 2009930578

Printed in the United States of America

iUniverse rev. date: 9/21/2009

PREFACE

There are times when people have experiences that they just want to share with interested readers for one reason or another. I have read several books that others have written with that intention, and have just had a happy experience which I probably would not have shared had it continued. But after a happy start, it had a sad ending, not just for me, but for several other people, as I will describe in the text. I had a wonderful job helping people as a case manager at Hope House in New Orleans as they were facing homelessness, and then was laid off, an event that simply should not have occurred. Ever since that event, I have thought about writing this book, about what to write in each chapter, about the happy experiences I have had, my love for New Orleans and what that city has meant for me for over 40 years, and why I felt I should share my experiences with the public.

Right at the outset, I would like to thank several people who were great companions to me throughout that year and thereafter, and who also gave me helpful hints when they learned about my intention to write this book. Here they are:

Brother Don Everard, Director of Hope House, who was a great supervisor and team leader and who always gave me good guidance as I did my job, as well as with my efforts to save the program or renew it.

Sister Lilliane Flavin, whom I was able to consult from time to time, and who often acted as a mother-figure at Hope House.

Joanika Davis, a great co-worker and friend who always had useful input as she and I did our work together, and whose friendship I will always cherish.

Denise Russell, manager of Jim Russell Records, whose friendship meant a lot to me, and who almost succeeded in saving our work with what almost was a helpful suggestion.

Action Reporter Bill Capo of Station WWL-TV who used his skills as a reporter in a way so as to almost help the program succeed, and who was supportive of my efforts as well.

My brother, Klaus-Christian Hofer, who gave me some useful hints as to the writing of this book.

And Mary Helen Lagasse, my Tulane friend, who also gave me some useful hints.

Morgan City, LA   THOMAS K. HOFER

MY NEW ORLEANS, TOO

No matter where anyone is born and raised, whenever he or she comes to New Orleans, he or she is in for a special experience. And I am no exception.

I was born March 2, 1947, in Vienna, Austria. In 1955, when I was eight years old, my parents, my younger brother, Klaus, and I moved to Giessen, Germany, when my father became an instructor of zoology at the university there. My memories of these two cities are happy ones, and for a long time, I thought I would spend the rest of my life in Giessen. I remember that in 1960, when I was in the seventh grade at school there, I started learning English. I enjoyed my lessons in English very much; also, my first English teacher was an exceptional scholar in British heritage. She knew that subject like the palm of her hand. She had spent time in Seattle, Washington, as well. Also, at the time I lived in Giessen, that city was in the American sector of what was then West-Germany, and the American soldiers had a good relationship with

1

the people of whatever city they were stationed at. Giessen was no exception. I also remember my fascination with the American automobiles and how fancy they were when compared to the simple German automobiles. The simplest American automobile I remember was the Jeep which the soldiers used quite frequently but which soon became a civilian automobile used by Germans as well.

My father made his first trip to the United States in November 1963. The day of his return coincided with the day John F. Kennedy was shot. After his return, my father called himself the best English speaker of the family. Then, in June of 1964, he brought a young American student to our home. She did not speak any German, so she and he spoke in English. I listened for a while, then decided to take my own crack at speaking, and was surprised at my own ability to speak. My father had long planned for all of us to come to the United States, and had concerns about how we would communicate; but I convinced him that I could indeed speak English well enough to make it. I had all along done my own exercises in formulating sentences in English, and that turned out to be more helpful than I even thought it would.

The next year, on 29 August 1965, the entire family came to the United States. We boarded a Lufthansa German Airlines Boeing 707 in Frankfurt and flew to New York. Then it took us almost three hours to change planes, and we then flew from New York nonstop to New Orleans. Our day that day was 31 hours long. Some friends met us in New Orleans, and took us to Covington, where my father had received a research associateship at the Delta Regional Primate Research Center of Tulane University. I already knew at the time of our trip that I would soon have to move to New Orleans and enter school at Tulane University, and after Hurricane Betsy rendered us without electricity for two days, our friends took me to Tulane. I spent an entire week in orientation, with the daughter of our friends assisting me. At first, I was a bit shy as I became acquainted with the campus, and did not do much getting around in New Orleans. But, with the daughter of our friends guiding me around, I soon learned how to use the St. Charles streetcar to go to downtown New Orleans.

After a week's orientation, including a strenuous registration process, classes started at Tulane, and I soon realized that things were not like they were in Germany. But then again, I had grown tired of the very antiquated German school system, and so I went into the American school system with an open mind. And the more I listened to the lectures in English and communicated in English with the professors, students, and other University personnel, the more fluent in English I became. Sure, I had a substantial knowledge of English grammar and vocabulary before coming to the United States; still, being exposed to the language 24 hours a day made a big difference.

My first trip to downtown New Orleans occurred on

13 October 1965. Philip Matthew Hannan, heretofore Auxiliary Bishop of Washington, had just been appointed Archbishop of New Orleans, and his installation was set for that day at St. Louis Cathedral. So I took the St. Charles streetcar downtown, and was fascinated by the ride. St. Charles Avenue was already at that time a most attractive street, and I enjoyed seeing the old buildings, the churches, and other sites. Among the major avenues that the trolley crossed were Nashville Avenue, Jefferson Avenue, Napoleon Avenue (which reminded me of the fact that New Orleans had a French heritage, so naming a street after that famous French leader seemed appropriate to me), Louisiana Avenue, Washington Avenue, Jackson Avenue, and Lee Circle (which I knew all along was named after Robert E. Lee). Finally, the trolley reached Canal Street, and I exited it and walked to Chartres Street and ultimately to the cathedral. Of course, the church was full of clergy and laity. The installation service went well; then I had coffee and doughnuts at the Café du Monde which I had known about before. Then I took another trolley back to the campus. But I had a good view of the French Quarter, and was fascinated by it. The old buildings with their balconies and wrought-iron fences looked very European to me, so I soon felt at home not only in the French Quarter but soon in all of New Orleans. From then on, I used the St. Charles street car when going downtown until some students told me about the Freret Street bus which also went downtown. From then on, I

took that bus most of the time, because that bus crossed through the campus, just as Freret Street itself does, and when returning from downtown New Orleans, I was able to exit the bus and go straight to my dorm. The Freret Street bus crossed through some poor neighborhoods of New Orleans, but I was not very phased by that; I only thought of Tulane, where I lived, and downtown, where I had to go for whatever reason. The Freret Street route was not as attractive as the St. Charles route.

One day, after a brief downtown errand, I saw a bus marked "Tulane", and boarded it, intending to go back to Tulane University and thinking that that was its destination, too. Although I soon realized that it went a totally different route, I remained on it. It went through a long street, which I soon learned was Tulane *Avenue*, and then suddenly turned onto a small street until it reached a red light. At that light, it made a left turn onto a big street which I later learned was Carrollton Avenue. After several blocks, it ended on the corner of Carrollton and Claiborne Avenues, and I recognized Claiborne Avenue as the northern border of the Tulane campus. I asked the driver how to get from the stop to the Tulane campus. He gave me the directions, and I made it to the Tulane campus well in time to have my lunch at the Bruff Commons Dining Hall. I often thought of that cute error I made, however, I never again boarded the Tulane bus again with the intention of going from downtown back to Tulane University.

From then on, I took either the St. Charles trolley or the Freret bus when going downtown.

New Orleans always impressed me as a city rich in heritage and history, and that's what I liked about it the most. I always had a love for heritage and history, and that is what made me feel right at home in that city. Of course, already at that time, the Tulane University campus itself had both old and modern buildings. The section between St. Charles Avenue and Freret Street was full of the old buildings, however, between Freret and Willow Streets, there were both old and modern buildings, Newcomb Hall, Dixon Hall, McAlister Auditorium, the observatory and several other old buildings, along with the modern University Center and the modern dormitory buildings. North of Willow Street was, of course, the Tulane Stadium, the several athletic buildings and fields, and on the northern edge of the campus, there was Charles Rosen House, the married student's dorm.

In my first year at Tulane, I did not do a lot of walking around the neighborhood, except that I visited Audubon Park from time to time. I was very disappointed with the Audubon zoo which at that time was in very poor shape (it has since vastly improved), however, the park itself was attractive, and reminded me of several attractive parks I had seen in Austria and Germany. When I fist saw the zoo, I was so disappointed by it that I decided not to mention it to my family members, however, they visited it later, and came away with the same opinion.

After a three-month summer stay in Covington with my parents and brother, I returned to New Orleans for another year of study at Tulane, and this time decided to make walks through the University section. The neighborhood was most attractive to me; I enjoyed the buildings and the trees that lined the streets. I came across several sites within that neighborhood, and at one point, came across the Maple Street Book Shop through which I browsed quite a bit when I first saw it. I actually thought that it had been there for a long time, however, I later learned that it was not opened until 1964, the year before I came to the United States. Still, it had a lot of good books, and I was able to use some for my studies. And I later learned that the store often was used even by Tulane professors as they ordered textbooks for their classes, because those professors preferred that store over the Tulane Bookstore.

I enjoyed taking the busses through New Orleans, and seeing more and more of the city. And I soon learned that the neighborhoods of New Orleans differed almost one from another. I noticed a great difference between the University area and the Lakeview area the first time I went to Lakeview; also, when I went to visit a friend at the New Orleans Baptist Theological Seminary, I noticed a great deal of difference there as well. I could go on and on, giving one example after another. But New Orleans soon became my American hometown.

Even after moving back in with my parents in Covington and transferring to Southeastern Louisiana College in Hammond in 1967, I still thought a lot about New Orleans; in fact, I missed it. I used every chance I could get to go there for visits. And in the summer of 1968, I went to stay in the guest room of the Tulane Baptist Student Center and have a summer job in New Orleans. That was yet another joyful experience.

I spent one more year at Southeastern, then dropped out, had two jobs in New Orleans, attended the Tulane Summer School in 1970, and then had one business job, again in New Orleans. After first commuting between Covington and New Orleans, I moved back to New Orleans in April 1971, again being back in my beloved city. One month later, I re-enrolled at Tulane University, but because I had a job during the day, I had to register for evening classes. And after half a year of downtown jobs, in January 1972, I started a job at the Tulane University Library as an assistant librarian. So that put me full-scale at Tulane, and because of my taking night classes there, that suited me fine, especially since I had moved to the University area of the city.

There is a lot about New Orleans that I have not as yet addressed. New Orleans is, of course, the birthplace of jazz, and from time to time, I was able to visit Preservation Hall so as to listen to some of it. I was able to see several jazz performers in other locations as well, and they all made me appreciate jazz music. I remembered one classmate I had in secondary school in Germany who was a jazz fan for a long time; he would have felt right at home in New Orleans. I myself have been a fan of country music, some rock music, and since 1971, when I saw my first performance of Handel's "Messiah", classical music as well. But jazz also meant a lot to me, and still does, because it is part of New Orleans history.

Heritage and history are landmarks of New Orleans. St. Louis Cathedral is the oldest cathedral in all of the United States, and the entire French Quarter has a historic flavor to it. As often as I have bee in the quarter, I enjoyed the old shops on Royal Street, the Café du Monde, the French Market, the Cabildo, the Presbytere, and a lot of other old buildings. Being a European native, I felt right at home in New Orleans at all times. Of course, when I learned all about the United States in my world geography lessons in Germany, I learned that there were a lot of other historic cities in the United States, such as Boston, New York, Philadelphia, Baltimore, Washington, D. C., San Antonio, St. Louis, and others. And my father had made two trips to the United States before we all came, and on both trips, he visited some of those cities himself.

Another landmark of New Orleans that I became acquainted with was Mardi Gras. I knew from the very first that Mardi Gras was a carnival-type celebration in which people could have fun one last time before the solemn Lenten season. And back in Germany, carnival, known as Fasching in that country, was celebrated just as Mardi Gras. I remember the start of that carnival every

November 11, the introduction of the prince and princess, and then the so-called cap sessions which were held in roast-style. I enjoyed these the most. Because we came to New Orleans in 1965, I witnessed my first Mardi Gras in 1966, and first missed the cap sessions. But I figured that other than that, Mardi Gras would suit me fine. Mardi Gras 1967, I regret to say, was another story. I was still living in a Tulane dorm, and there was a gang of students who were rowdies to begin with. At Mardi Gras time, they invited some of their friends from their hometowns to come to New Orleans, and there were eight people sleeping in a room designed for two only. These students and their guests then went to the French Quarter, polluted themselves with alcohol to the brim, raced back to the campus, and destroyed everything in their paths. It got to the point where the senior advisor in the dorm issued a warning that if another disturbance or destruction of property occurred, all guests would have to leave. I managed to stay away from this wild crowd, but often was harassed by some of them for not "having fun." From then on, I tended to skip Mardi Gras because of the bad taste I had gotten from it. First, I would just stay in Covington and go to the parade there, then I would just stay in my apartment and not go out until Ash Wednesday.

Another critical observation I made was that Lent was not fully observed, but that parades were held on St. Patrick and St. Joseph's Days. That seemed reprehensible to me; in my opinion, these parades were just a Mardi Gras continuation, and interfered with Lent. I remember being with one of my friends on a balcony in New Orleans, watching such a parade, and she and I were wondering how the local clergy felt about such going on during the Lenten season. As it turns out, to this day, not one clergyman has taken a stand on this.

Once back at Tulane, both working and studying, I enjoyed the college atmosphere, and even though working during the day and studying at night was hard at times, I did not mind that. I enjoyed myself doing things pretty much on my own. From time to time, as I was able to do, I spent weekends with my parents in Covington (my younger brother, Klaus, who had also come with us in 1965 and graduated from Covington High School in 1967, left us in January 1970 after an ill-fated marriage to an American woman), and otherwise enjoying life as I saw fit. Finally, on May 15, 1976, I received my Bachelor of Arts degree, so that ended my going to classes in the evening after work. The next year, my parents decided to move back to Germany, and because I had friends in Mid-City of New Orleans, I moved there, and had barely set up my own place there when I had to make trip after trip to Covington to assist my parents until they finally left in December 1977.

From then on, I was totally by myself. One year later, my brother, Klaus, called to tell me he had just moved to Halifax, Nova Scotia, Canada. I remained working at the Tulane Library until May 1979 when I landed a job as an Eligibility Worker with the State of Louisiana, Office of Family Security (a/k/a welfare department). This, of course, was the beginning of my social service career, and in college, I had majored in political science and minored in English and Spanish; this new job made me feel as if I should have majored in sociology. This was my first job working with the public, and at the beginning, I was full of questions as to how to deal with that. At one individual interview, at which I was ultimately hired, I was made aware of the fact that the clients I was having to deal with had gotten themselves into troublesome situations, and that I was expected to help them out of these situations. After I was hired, I had to go to Baton Rouge for a three-week training session (I was able to return to New Orleans for the weekends), and the trainers did a splendid job in teaching. Then, I had to report to my office, located at 2601 Tulane Avenue, a block away from the intersection of Tulane and Broad, and first learn some local routines. I was then assigned to a supervisor whom I had a lot of respect for. He was very good at issuing guidelines and training me further. I also scheduled my first interviews, which began the following week. In my first interview, I was clumsy, and also was anxious about making sure I did not omit anything. It lasted an hour, because I kept stopping and thinking. I often wondered what my client thought about my way of doing that interview. When she told me six months later how good she felt about me, I disclosed to her that six months earlier, she was the first client I ever interviewed. She got a real laugh about it, and told me she did not mind my being clumsy at that time. With all my other clients, I managed to work well from the start.

Of course, working in welfare was challenging in a number of ways, and confronted me with situations that I had heretofore not known about. I was used to families with a father and a mother; now I had to deal with single moms who entangled themselves in intimate relationships resulting in pregnancies and childbirths, mothers having children from several fathers, some mothers not even being able to name a father for a child because they had several relationships resulting in pregnancies, and so forth. Also, some of these mothers had no high school diplomas, had dropped out of high school in the ninth grade or lower, and were, therefore, barely employable. I was familiar with the phrase "To get a good job, get a good education."

Another thing I learned was that the welfare mothers were caught in a vicious cycle because those who lived in the HANO-operated housing projects wanted to get out due to the unsafe conditions, and those who lived in private housing were often facing eviction because they could not pay the rent. As for the housing projects, I had heard about them before starting the job, but not in all detail. In fact, when taking the Freret Street bus downtown and then back to Tulane, I passed by the Magnolia Street project without noticing the similar looking buildings. Then, in 1970, the Desire Housing project made the news in New Orleans when the Black Panthers staged an uprising in that project. And in 1973, a young student nurse, Jo Ellen Smith, entered the Fischer project in Algiers to visit a patient, and as she left the patient, she was raped and killed. Both incidents were reported at length in the media; still, the reports did not give the insights into what life in a project was like in the way in which I learned about them as I started my welfare worker's job. One thing I learned right at the outset is that there is no such thing as a good project. New Orleans had nine such projects, and they could best be divided into the barely acceptable ones, with some exception, and the ones that were totally unacceptable. From what I learned from those of my clients living in these projects, life in at least some of them was pure hell. They told me of drug deals, shootings, robberies, and other crimes going on. Some were scared to live there but had no other choice, because they could not afford any other place to stay. They were afraid for their children and for themselves. Now, I do not mean to suggest that the projects were full of derelicts and undesirables; in fact, two people I had associations with lived in the somewhat acceptable projects. But I often asked myself how a parent could raise a child in an environment full of drug deals and shootings. At one point, a client told me that she was instructed by the local project office that she would have to come to the office to sign her lease as it would not be mailed; I suggested that she tell that office to provide her with a bullet-proof vest so that she could make it safely back and forth.

To be sure, a client could never choose which project to live in. Instead, anyone wanting to seek housing had to apply to the Housing Authority of New Orleans (HANO) for a residence; then HANO would locate a residence in any project that was available, and the client then had no choice but to accept it. HANO, of course, also administered the Section 8 program which provided for paying rent to private landlords so that clients could live in private housing and only pay a small portion of the rent, but that program often ran out of money, and the waiting list was mostly very long. Another alternative were the so-called scatter site homes where HANO would charge low rent, however, the client also had to pay utilities on a separate basis.

I again want to point out that my trainers for the job were excellent, however, they failed in one aspect: the establishing of a good working relationship with the clients. They dwelled too heavily on the aspect of clients complaining about what we would do, no matter how well we did our jobs. Had I just listened to them, I would have come away with the impression of never being able to please any client. But I took my own approach to the worker-client relationship. I contemplated of what I would expect whenever I walked into any agency or office for some service; namely, I would expect attention, courtesy, and professionalism. I then figured to make it a point of treating my clients the same way, no matter how different their lifestyle was from mine. Certainly there were differences; still, my clients were human beings like me, and as such, they had the same expectations that I had. So I made it a point of extending proper courtesy when meeting a client, also having a friendly attitude, and doing my best to provide service as best as I could. And I can state in good conscience that I came a long way like that, as my supervisor noted that he received few calls from them about me.

Although the manner in which clients became dependent upon welfare varied, I noticed that a sizeable majority tended to deliberately get into that system by having intimate relationships outside of marriage resulting in childbirths and then needing support. I remember how a woman told me when I asked her how she became pregnant that she and the man "just went to bed together – it just happened." Another woman told me she was "just on the streets, messing around" and then could not even name a father for her expectant baby. Both of these situations seemed reprehensible to me, but I could not easily scold these women. I simply suggested family planning and birth control for them. On another occasion, a woman who just had a baby told me she may be pregnant again. When I asked her if she had entangled herself in yet another relationship, she replied, "Mr. Hofer, I have to do something to get money for my children so as to buy clothes and toys for them." I then gave her several referrals for outlets where she could get these items without the relationships. Another thing I dreaded were all these teenagers getting pregnant; I felt sorry for their children, since these mothers were not mature enough to deal with a child. Although some of these children ended up getting in trouble with the law, there were several others who manage to scramble out of these miserable conditions and become very productive citizens. And yet another thing: not all these welfare recipients were black; I had several white clients as well.

I realize that I digressed from the theme of New Orleans and why I fell in love with that city, but this was an insertion that I felt I had to make, given the fact that there was, and is to this very day, a lot of talk about welfare recipients and their lifestyle.

After my parents left in 1977, I remained in New Orleans, living by myself. I had a very pleasant neighbor who lived with her teenage daughter in the apartment below mine (we are still good friends) as well as several women with whom I had dating relationships. One, a Peruvian, invited me for several dates while living in New Orleans until October 1981 when she suddenly packed up, and left for Peru. Then in 1982, she suddenly returned to New Orleans, and again invited me to date her for a concert. It was the week before Memorial Day that year, and on that day I wanted to take her to yet another concert, but she was not able to make it. I then decided to go by myself.

But then an event occurred that changed things completely for me for the next 21 years. On Sunday before Memorial Day, I attended church and assisted at the service, then went to the reception hall for coffee and doughnuts. I made myself a cup of coffee, then walked back to the entrance when it suddenly opened, and a woman whom I had not seen before walked in. Inasmuch as she was a visitor, I decided to introduce myself and make her welcome at the church. We talked a lot, then exchanged our names and addresses (her name was Donna Lyn Pence), and then she agreed to go out with me to that concert which was held on Memorial Day in New Orleans City Park. Our dating relationship went on and on, and what I kept noticing was that she kept joining me at church every Sunday, something my previous dates never did. Soon I met her parents who lived in New Orleans all along (they were active Episcopalians), and one on occasion, Donna, her parents, and I went to Baton Rouge where we met her brother and his family; his youngest child, Jonathan, was celebrating his fourth birthday that day.

When I realized that Donna's and my relationship was close to resulting in marriage, I went through some extensive soul searching and reviewing of my past to see if I indeed was ready for that major step. I went all the way to my Roman Catholic background to see if I did not want to become a celibate priest after all. But I soon eliminated that; still, I realized that a marital relationship was far more that just a casual dating relationship. Then, while this was going on, Donna wanted the two of us speak to an Episcopal priest whom I had known all along about this situation. I agreed to make that appointment. Just at the same time, the father of one of my best friends died. He had been sick for several days, and was even in the hospital. Donna and I went to see him, however, he had just been taken to a treatment room for an angiogram to which he did not react well. Donna, as I noticed, did a splendid job in comforting his wife; I agonized with the family and was not all that well at comforting. The next day, the old man died. The funeral took place a few days later, and Donna joined me, along with my pleasant neighbor whom she had met before. My neighbor agonized at the funeral, since it reminded her of her mother's death in early 1979.

I was not exactly in the best spirits, either, but Donna again kept up her spirits, and was a great companion to my neighbor and myself. This then finally convinced me that Donna was indeed able to be a capable wife in the sense of Proverbs 31:10, so when we met with the priest a few days later, I proposed. She was surprised, but afterwards I told her what gave me the idea that she would indeed make a good wife for me.

A few weeks later, I met her children from her previous marriage, which ended in divorce when she found her previous husband in bed with another woman. I spent Christmas that year in Germany with my mother, then, after coming back, we went straight ahead with the wedding plans and got married 20 May 1983 in a lovely ceremony at Grace Episcopal Church in New Orleans. My younger brother, Klaus, came from Canada with his second wife, Paula, to be present. He and she were married 29 August 1981, and I went to their wedding all the while thinking that eventually I would get married, too, but to whom? The answer came about a year later when Donna and I became engaged. Our wedding took place 20 May 1983 in the evening, and we had a reception that lasted well into the late evening. After Donna and I changed into go-away clothes, we then took my brother and sister-in-law to the newly-built Sheraton Canal hotel, then made out way to the Hilton Airport Inn across the street from the airport.

The next day, Klaus and Paula joined us for breakfast at the Hilton. After that, we checked out and went to the airport to meet my in-laws and Donna's children from her previous marriage. Donna and I then flew to Dallas where we met her brother and sister-in-law. The next day, we flew to Hawaii for a one-week honeymoon, first spending four days on Oahu Island where Honolulu is, then three days on Maui Island where we went sightseeing in a rented car. After that, we flew back to New Orleans. We had to get used to married life, as our paths which were different before the wedding day, had now joined, and we would have to face good and bad times together. But I can say in good conscience that we lived a successful married life.

I continued my job in the Office of Family Security, however, the next year, I almost quit. Donna had gotten pregnant, and we were expecting twins. I realized then that I would become a father and had to take additional responsibility as the children would be looking to Donna and me for love, guidance, leadership, discipline, and nurture. And that you do not learn from a simple dating relationship. However, Donna's pregnancy was difficult from the very first, and that had me worried. I had looked forward to our twins, however, one day I came home to find her in total distress. She had come home from the doctor, and had a miscarriage at that visit. After spending time with her, I called the rector (pastor) of the church we attended, and he came by to spend time and say a prayer with us. The next day, I took an entire day off to be with Donna.

The miscarriage had me frustrated. And it kept me thinking of all these babies that were born to welfare mothers in at times most undesirable conditions. Also I kept thinking that if Donna and I had these twins, or if we would have had another child, that child would have known its mother and father at all times. Donna herself was not able to look at a newborn infant for a long time, and even I had difficulty with that. But I tend to go on with my life, so I eventually was able to get through with these feelings. Actually, when Donna and I were married, I was working in the refugee program where I did not have to deal with these many babies. But the agony and frustration never went totally away. The doctors told Donna never to try for another baby as she would not be able to handle it, so she and I agreed that our marriage would be childless.

I still held on to my job in the Office of Family Security, and still noticed the illegitimate births. However, at one point, some Child Welfare League put out some posters campaigning against teenage pregnancy. One especially caught my attention. It showed a sad-looking teenage girl with a baby on her lap and an inscription over it reading, "It's like being grounded for 18 years." I felt that that poster told it like it is.

Another big topic that came up during those years was welfare reform. In 1984, Ronald Reagan had just been re-elected President, and he was big into that, however, he had started reforms that had no good results; in fact, some had to be reversed. The welfare rolls did not diminish, and I could easily tell that, because our caseloads did not decrease; in fact, they increased. However, one good thing that came out of these reforms: child support laws were toughened, and those deadbeat dads who thought they could just have an easy ride with having sex and fathering children and then simply walking away from the relationships learned that that foolish behavior was not going to be tolerated. I had believed all along that these absent parents should face responsibility, and now salaries could be attached, income tax refunds could be withheld, driver's licenses could be taken, and other measures could be taken to enforce child support. That all met with my full approval.

"Welfare reform" actually meant that mothers would put their children into day care centers which were government subsidized, and then seek employment. That was fine for me in itself as well, however, there were, and still are, some difficulties. For one thing, some of these mothers did not even have a high school diploma or GED and/or no job skills. Additionally, even when they were on their jobs and had their children in day care, whenever the children became ill, the mothers, not the day care centers, had to take the children to the doctor. And private employers oftentimes would not look too kindly on mothers taking off from work for this or any other reason. At times, this would result in the mothers being terminated from their jobs, and then they would have to get back on welfare all over again.

The "bottom line" is that the welfare system, as it was incepted, should never have been developed that way.

Donna, of course, had her two children from her previous marriage, Cindy and Auston IV. After we got married, we wanted both of these children back with us. They were with their father and stepmother, and they had a hard time getting along in that home. So we started legal proceedings, however, what eventually occurred was that the father gave us Cindy but kept his son, and we could do nothing about that. We provided Cindy with a loving home, put her in school, and went on with our lives. Cindy, however, soon met a young man, and had a baby, Katherine Lyn, with him. Earlier, Cindy also gave us a dog, Nookie, whom she got out of a litter. Donna and I took the dog as well, and once the baby was born, she became very much part of our lives. At first, she was all her time at home, however, when Donna needed major surgery, Katherine, "Katie" as we called her, was placed in a day care center. That turned out to be most useful for her.

Donna and I enjoyed New Orleans throughout that whole time. Oftentimes, we took outings, taking a bus to downtown New Orleans and walking through the French Quarter; sometimes we shopped, sometimes we just browsed around. One of her favorite stores was Krauss; she had been used to that store from her childhood days, when she and one of her long-time friends went there all the time. Donna was a New Orleans native and grew up in the University area; as such, she had been to the Tulane campus several times. Of course, she knew of my Tulane past, my attending Tulane until I graduated from there as well as my past employment there as well. Her parents still lived in an old house on Arabella Street, within walking distance of the campus. I myself went to the campus several times to get a haircut at the Tulane barber shop. The barber there had been employed when I first came to Tulane in 1965, and still remembered how I had told him of my coming with my parents and brother that year. Oftentimes, I would also go to the library, as some of my old acquaintances were still working there.

In 1984, Donna and I had a most enjoyable experience. My uncle and aunt, Dr. and Mrs. Ewalt Lesch, who lived in a little town just south of my native Vienna, came to visit us in the course of a world trip. They had started that trip in Halifax, Nova Scotia, Canada, then traveled to New York; then they came to visit us in New Orleans. They were fascinated by what they saw in New Orleans, especially with the richness of heritage and history. We showed them the French Quarter, St. Louis Cathedral, the Cabildo, and the Presbytere; then we took them to the steamer NATCHEZ for a cruise. The next day, we showed them the Tulane campus and Uptown New Orleans; afterwards, it was on to the Deutsches Haus for the Oktoberfest. The next day, we took them to Covington and St. Joseph's Abbey and to the Missisippi Gulf Coast. And on the following day, they left for Mexico. Their trip then took them to San Francisco, Hawaii, Fiji, New Zealand, Australia, Bali, Yoctjakarta, Hong Kong, Macao, India, Egypt, and back home to Austria.

Donna and I respected each other's needs to see our friends from the time before we were married. She had an old friend, Evelyn Robins, whom she grew up with. She and Evelyn kept going on outings to shop and spend time, and she loved to shop, more so than I did. I had an old friend, Gamil Makari, who worked with me at the Tulane Library. He was Best Man at out wedding (Evelyn was Matron of Honor), and he and I often took outings to the French Quarter which ended with coffee and doughnuts at the Café du Monde. In 1984, our shopping abilities were increased as the old Jackson Brewery, which had been left abandoned after it shut down, was converted into a shopping center. There was a newsstand where I was able to buy German magazines and newspapers. Gamil, of course, was not my only friend, there was Julia Fuentes, who, with her daughter, Eslie, was my neighbor until she moved to Metairie in early 1983. Another old friend of mine, Gasper Gilardi, who had attended Southeastern with me from 1967 to 1969, also maintained contact with me and took me on outings. Donna and I were happy with these friends. And their contacts never interfered with our marital relationship.

In 1987, another election for Governor of Louisiana had to be held. Edwin W. Edwards was on the verge of completing his third term. He had promised to make reforms and to upgrade the state, however, once he became governor, he realized that the state did not have the resources to do these upgrades. Tax increases simply did not do the trick; the state had lost revenue due to the collapse of the world oil market. In fact, we were facing drastic budget cuts which almost meant my losing my job. We campaigned hard to avert these cuts, and I wrote to the governor myself, and received a reply from him which I then shared with my co-workers. Eventually, the cuts were never made, so we could go on with our lives and jobs.

But the election made a difference. There were lots of candidates for Governor, and on election day, the people voted. The polls closed at 8:00 p. m.; and we were able to see some results while attending a Tulane football game. Buddy Roemer, whom the papers and others endorsed for whatever reason, took an early lead, with the incumbent Edwin Edwards trailing him. We returned home from the game and continued watching the results. It soon became clear that there would have to be a runoff between Roemer and Edwards. Then, at about midnight, Edwards suddenly came down and announced in a very somber and subdued mood that he would not continue the race, thus in effect giving the post to Roemer. The same Mr. Edwards who so triumphantly had promised to turn this state around had to admit that the state was in deep financial straits stemming from the loss of oil revenue.

Although I eventually did not believe Edwards' promises after some time of his being governor for the third time, I was genuinely impressed with some of his appointees, such as Dr. Sandra Robinson, secretary of the Department of Health and Human Resources, as well as some of the officials that worked with her. And when you have a state job, you would want to have people over you whom you can trust when working at the grassroots. Now we were facing a new governor and a new cabinet officer for DHHR as well, and that caused some concern.

Buddy Roemer took office in March of 1988, and soon showed that he was unable to deal with the financial situation. Additionally, at least in my opinion, he seemed to want dictatorial powers to do as he pleased. For example, when he wanted to cut the budget, he asked the legislature to give him the power to "cut as I want". I was one of several people who did not want this, so I contacted my legislators protesting this and asking them not to grant Roemer that power. They and the entire legislature ignored that, Roemer got his wish, and a lot of people were affected by those cuts. Additionally, the next year, per his executive order, state employees were paid twice a month instead of being paid bi-weekly as before; this was said to be a saving measure. I, for one had a hard time making ends meet and supporting my family. Additionally, I became uncomfortable with the Roemer administration and its shenanigans.

Donna and I had friends in Winter Springs, Florida (just outside of Orlando), and we shared our concerns with them. They in turn contacted the State of Florida's Department of Health and Rehabilitative Services, and I received a job application form. Also, we received several brochures and pamphlets from several apartment complexes in the Orlando area, and after I completed and returned the application form, I received a notice asking me to come for an appointment. Donna and I then went by bus from New Orleans to Orlando and stood with our friends. The next day I went for the interview, and it went well. We spent an entire week looking for a place to stay until we found an apartment complex in southwest Orlando that we liked. We also did a lot of sightseeing before we returned after a week.

After we returned, I spent three months reflecting on

the fact that I had to leave my beloved New Orleans just to continue my career in social service which I was also happy with. But I continued distrusting Governor Roemer and continued to be unhappy with his administration and his cabinet. Then, in early August, a supervisor from the Florida Department of Health and Rehabilitative Services called me to tell me I was hired for the job as Public Assistance Specialist, and we agreed that September 11, 1989, would be my starting date. Then Donna and I re-contacted the apartment complex that we had settled upon, and made a deposit. My last day at work in Louisiana was August 25, 1989. Then we packed, and I flew to Orlando on 6 September 1989, set up a bank account, and started work September 11 as planned. I stood with our friends for two weeks after starting the job until Donna joined me. She had bought a station wagon which our landlord wanted to sell, and she came in it, accompanied by Cindy, my stepdaughter, and Katie, my grandchild. Cindy and Katie returned to New Orleans two days later.

I recall that before we came to the United States, an English teacher I had in school in Germany suggested that I, after arriving in New Orleans, make trips to other cities in the United States, as the cities in the United States differ quite a bit from each other. And I actually had made visits to other cities – Atlanta, San Antonio, Dallas, Houston, Austin, and Honolulu, just to name some. Still, New Orleans and Orlando are poles apart. One thing I soon learned is that Orlando is all about tourism. I learned that after World War II, the space industry, located in nearby Cape Canaveral, brought jobs to Central Florida. Still, Orlando was virtually unknown until 1971 when Disney World was opened. (I learned about that opening that year while working for an insurance company that opened a regional office in Orlando.) From then on, Orlando ballooned. But what I noticed was the whereas New Orleans decorated itself on several occasions in that Mardi Gras soon followed Christmas, Easter soon followed Mardi Gras, and so forth, Orlando just decorated itself for Christmas; otherwise, the city was plain. It soon occurred to me that the city had little heritage and history. When I shared that observation with an Orlando resident, she replied, "The history of Orlando is divided up into the pre-Mickey era and the post-Mickey era." Orlando was a "cold glory", as my mother would have called it. And I soon started to miss New Orleans, its charm, its heritage, and its tradition. I remember buying my first CD player, and one of the first CD's that Donna and I bought was one by Harry Connick, Jr., and his song "Do you know what it means to miss New Orleans." And every time we made trips back to New Orleans, we thought of the happy times we spent there. Of course, we had good things going for us in Orlando, too; I had a good job in child protection, and we made some good friends there. There were stores we liked and other outlets. Still, it was nothing like New Orleans. In early 1997, family illnesses and other problems made us move back.

After we returned, it took me several months to find another job, but I finally landed a job at Covenant House New Orleans, first on a per-diem basis, but half a year later, the job became regular, and we were able to again settle in our own place. We first lived in a nice apartment complex in River Ridge, however, Cindy's boyfriend wanted to sell the house in Chalmette that he owned. My mother-in-law had died earlier that year, and we had to sell the house she was living in. Once that was accomplished, we bought the house in Chalmette and moved into it. I at first balked at buying a house, telling Donna that I had no manual skills and could not repair anything on my own, so repairs would cost a lot. But I soon agreed to the buying of the house. Our old friends were still around, and we enjoyed their companionship. And we once again enjoyed the beauty of New Orleans. And in November 1999, Donna and I finally were able to make a long-awaited trip to Germany and Austria; when we visited Vienna, she kept comparing it to New Orleans. After we returned and settled into New Orleans again, we joined St. Augustine's Episcopal Church in Metairie, and we enjoyed the fellowship we received there.

Then Donna's health deteriorated. She had strokes, beginning in 2001 and continuing thereafter. She had a hard time walking, could not do a lot of things she enjoyed, and was handicapped in every way. In April 2003 she suddenly lost all her strength in her legs as well as her walking ability; she could not even stand any more. She first was in a hospital, then in two nursing homes, again in a hospital, then home with home care, and finally died on her 60th birthday, 3 August 2003. I, of course, was devastated. The loving kindness she gave me, the good words, the support she gave me in good and bad times – all that was gone. What's worse, the day before her death, she was in the hospital, and I told her, "Honey, tomorrow, we will all be with you to celebrate your birthday." Instead, Cindy and I found ourselves in the office of the funeral director making plans for the burial which took place two days later. I received a lot of emotional support from friends, family members, and co-workers; still, the loss was hard to deal with.

After Donna's death, I soon realized that on my own, I could not maintain the house, given the fact that Donna and I had taken out two additional mortgages. So I had no choice but to sell it. After trying it on my own, I got hold of a realtor, Harriet Hyman, who owned her own realty company, RealtyDepot, Inc. I first moved into a lovely apartment complex a block away from St. Augustine's church; Harriet then continued to make efforts to sell the house, and finally, after a buyer was found, the house was sold March 31, 2004.

In that year, four of my best friends died. First came Jean Hunter, who was one of my friends from the Office of Family Security. She was a supervisor for the receptionists. She and I went to San Antonio in 1980 with a sowing club of which her sister, Jackie, was a lead member. She had several brothers and sisters. Her older brother, Frank, often acted like the patriarch of the family, but in a caring and loving way. Jean and I often exchanged thoughts about our jobs and the welfare situation. At her funeral, the entire family was present, and I felt very privileged to be on hand for her farewell.

Next to die was my old friend, Gasper Gilardi. He and I were good friend when he and I attended Southeastern in Hammond. He was quite different from the white supremacist crowd that I encountered there and which consistently antagonized me with "Heil Hitler", "Bring us another Hitler to get rid of the niggers" and other such slogans. He knew of my foreign background and was very open-minded. He respected every human being, regardless of race, color, or creed. Often, he would take a very open stand against racial prejudice. In his last years, he was sick throughout, and his health deteriorated ongoingly. I remember when he attended Donna's wake; I was so shocked at his appearance that I forgot my own grief for a while. The next year, April 1, 2004, he was brought to the hospital with a heart attack. I visited him the next day in the CCU. The following day, I came again for another visit, and he bemoaned the fact that he was not able to treat me to dinner at his home for Easter Sunday. I assured him that I would make it to the hospital instead and spend Easter with him. We exchanged a few more words, then I had to leave. The next day, Good Friday, I decided to put in a morning visit since I had to be at church for the noon service of Good Friday, but when I arrived at the hospital, I learned that he had passed away. The Good Friday service was for me a zig-zag route, dwelling on Jesus' death and Gasper's death, simultaneously. The funeral was held on Easter Monday, and I gave a brief, unprepared speech. A couple of days later, my realtor-friend, Harriet Hyman, called me to tell me she had known Gasper as well; while being a homebound teacher, he had taught one of her sons. I shared my experience with him with Harriet, talking about it for almost 30 minutes.

Constance H. Browne, who was one of my friends from St. Augustine's Church and who kept treating me for dinner at her home as often as she could, died a couple of weeks later. Then came Sherry DeMuth Chichester, one of my early Tulane friends. It was not until she died that I even learned that she was struggling with breast cancer.

In between these deaths, I did have a happy opportunity to share my love for New Orleans in a most unusual way. Shortly after joining St. Augustine's Episcopal Church, I also joined the Brotherhood of St. Andrew, a men's ministry which was founded in 1883 and of which my late father-in-law, Brewer F. Pence, was a lifelong member. Only two years later, in 2000, when new leadership was needed for our chapter, a new chapter director was elected, then I was elected vice-director of that same chapter. Two years later, 2002, the director decided that new leadership was needed, and I became director. Only a few months later, in July of that year, there was a National Council meeting of the entire Brotherhood scheduled to be held in Oviedo, Florida (another Orlando suburb), and I decided to make that meeting. That evening, I drove from Chalmette via I-10 all night long until I reached the junction I-10/I-75. Day had already broken when I reached that point, and so I continued driving until I reached the northern end of the Florida Turnpike which I entered to drive towards Orlando. After two other stops, I reached the Diocesan camp where the meeting was held, and had barely arrived for registration when the previous Diocesan Coordinator for Louisiana, Lincoln Lirette, simply handed me his post, stating he could no longer keep it for health reasons. The BStA's executive board consented to this action, so I agreed to take the position. At the meeting, I also learned that the next meeting, 2003, was to be held in Charleston, South Carolina. Then the Brotherhood was to move its meetings westward, however, no site was selected for the 2004 meeting. After some thought following my return, I then decided to invite the Brotherhood to come to New Orleans for that meeting, and my invitation was readily accepted. The preparatory work for that meeting was enormous, however, no one complained to me about my inviting that meeting without consulting anyone. I had taken an entire week off from my job, and was at the Chateau Sonesta Hotel (previously the site of the old D. H. Holmes department store) as early as July 6 to meet the first couple of guests that arrived for the meeting. The next day, the entire Executive Board met, then all the other out-of town guests arrived and checked in, and the meeting went well, better than I even expected. I succeeded in my endeavour to show New Orleans as a great place to visit, and all the guests loved to be here, and made their love for New Orleans known to me. That Saturday, three afternoon tours were held, one to the steamer Natchez for an afternoon cruise down and up the Mississippi which I escorted myself, another one to the D-Day museum, and another to Christ Church Cathedral. As I took the Natchez trip, I could tell what a great time the Brothers had aboard that paddlewheeler. I had recommended that they read Mark Twain's book *Life On The Mississippi* in which he describes his experiences as a riverboat captain; even I was startled when the on-board announcer stated that if Mark Twain were alive today, the Natchez would be his home. After our group returned to the hotel, we met with the people who went to the D-Day Museum as well as the people who went to the cathedral, and they also enjoyed their tours. One man told me how he went to the cathedral by St. Charles trolley, joined the cathedral tour, then walked from the cathedral to Magazine Street and saw various shops, then walked to the hotel. In his own words, he had a great time.

The Chateau Sonesta is, of course, located on Canal Street, and there area several shops in the vicinity. And a lot of the Brothers, along with their families, used every opportunity to shop for souvenirs. And the next day, when the meeting was over, a lot of guests, before departing, told me how great of a time they had in New Orleans. I rejoiced at succeeding in making my love for New Orleans known to others and having them have a good time in this city.

The next year, however, disaster struck, literally. After several previous hurricanes threatened New Orleans, Katrina came. I watched the news as that storm strafed the southern tip of the Florida peninsula and then roared through the golf. On August 27, when the storm approached New Orleans, I quickly filled up the gas tank in my car, then started some packing and securing in my apartment. I was still employed at Covenant House, and had to report for a night shift. While working that shift, I was given all the details on how we would evacuate to Houston, Texas, where there is another Covenant House. I ended the shift at 8:30 that morning, then went home, ate a quick breakfast, finished securing my apartment as best as I could, finished packing, and then drove back to Covenant House to assist in the evacuation. We met at 12:00 noon to finalize our plans, then left shortly after 2:00 p.m. We could not drive in a convoy, however, early that next day, August 29, we all arrived at Covenant House Texas in Houston. Day broke, and the director of Covenant House Texas addressed us. Then we turned on the TV's – and learned that the storm had devastated New Orleans. We learned of the 17th street canal breach and the water spilling into New Orleans from Lake Pontchartrian. We saw the pictures of the roof of the Superdome being torn by the storm and the windows of the Hyatt Regency Hotel having been broken. The cameras showed virtually total devastation. And we all were sad, depressed, and anxious about whether or not we even had a place to go back to. Most of us loved New Orleans, and it hurt us badly to see our beloved city in ruins like that. When I heard of the 17th street canal breach, I first thought it had breached into both Orleans and Jefferson Parishes, being on the parish line, however, an aerial view showed me that it only breached into Orleans Parish. Still, I was worried about Cindy, my stepdaughter, Katie, my oldest granddaughter, and Cindy's younger children, as they were living in Chalmette at that time. I was not able to reach them before evacuating, and worried myself sick. I was worried about my friends who lived in and around New Orleans, as at least some of them had lost everything, and possibly even their lives. When I attempted to make an Internet search, I learned that the computer lines were so jammed that there was no getting through. It was totally chaotic. The New Orleans Covenant House kids were first provisionally quartered in a large admission center, however, after a few days, Covenant House Texas fully admitted all of them into residence. The New Orleans staff was quartered into a hotel alongside an expressway.

I, after making an unsuccessful attempt on the Internet to locate my relatives, finally called my family in Morgan City, LA, where the father of my oldest grandchild was living. When I called the number, Jennie, the grandchild's stepmother, answered and expressed great relief at hearing my voice, as she was worried about me. She then assured me that Cindy, my stepdaughter, and the four children had evacuated. Of course, they lost everything they left behind, as Chalmette was totally flooded out. That Saturday, I made a FEMA claim, and I told the FEMA agent that I had good reason to believe that my apartment, which was on the third floor of the building, was damaged. By that time, Aaron Broussard, Jefferson Parish president, had given evacuated residents permission to return to check on their properties. I returned that Tuesday, and to my utter relief, found no damage, except that the food was totally spoiled and had to be thrown out. After some two hours of cleaning and packing an additional suitcase with items I wanted to take with me, I then drove to Morgan City where I met with Lenny, Katie's dad, Jennie, and her sister, Patrice "Patty" Ann. I first went to do my hygiene, then changed into comfortable clothes, fell asleep while watching TV, changed into my pajamas after waking up in the middle of the night, then, after breakfast, drove back to Houston. Upon arrival at the hotel, I learned that the Covenant House New Orleans director had come to Houston and told the New Orleans staff that Covenant House New Orleans would be fully operational in three months, and that the staff would have its jobs back. That moving date was then moved up to two months.

The pictures of the damage to New Orleans were depressing. It left us all in a saddened state of mind. My health deteriorated, both mentally and physically. My blood pressure rose to such an extent that I had to see a Texas doctor who wrote me off sick for two weeks and increased my medicine. While I was on sick leave, Hurricane Rita threatened Houston, so we had to evacuate westward to a ranch outside Columbus, Texas, located off I-10 towards San Antonio. We were able to return a few days later. Still, my mental state also deteriorated. I was having crying and shaking spells. At one point, after I was given a Bible, I was not able to open it to Psalm 23 as that psalm speaks of green pastures and still waters. "Waters" reminded me of the picture of the breach of the 17th street canal which spilled all the water into New Orleans, and these waters also destroyed a lot of beautiful green grass that enhanced the beauty of New Orleans. The first lines of Psalm 22 ("My God, my God, why have you forsaken me?") and 130 ("Out of the depths I cry to Thee, O Lord.") kept flashing across my mind almost all the time. And at first, I dreaded staying in Houston, however, the New Orleans staff was soon moved to an apartment complex close to the Astrodome. I then located a church that I could attend, St. John The Divine Episcopal Church, located on Westheimer Road, and the fellowship there was great. I was treated with kindness when I told the people that I was an evacuee from New Orleans.

The news media did a splendid job in reporting what was going on in New Orleans after the storm. The national media – ABC, CBS, CNN, and NBC – constantly kept reporting on the conditions in that city. Additionally, the local newspaper, the HOUSTON CHRONICLE, did an equally splendid job in keeping us informed. For example, when the Café du Monde was reopened, the Chronicle reported on that event. In between, New Orleans artists made performances on TV to promote New Orleans. For example, at one point, Harry Connick, Jr. sang "Way down yonder in New Orleans." A lot of us wondered, would New Orleans ever rise to be that beautiful city again that it was before the storm?

A lot of books were written about the storm and what it did to New Orleans and the Mississippi Gulf Coast. Most showed pictures of the disaster, and I soon could not look at them any more, having seen the flooding pictures day by day on TV as well as in the Chronicle and USA Today. When House Speaker Dennis Hastert suggested that New Orleans never be rebuilt and left in the damaged state, that prompted a writer to write *Why New Orleans Matters,* describing why the city is important to the country and the world, and therefore had to be rebuilt.

I did not read that book but came across another book entitled *My New Orleans,* a collection of articles written by several persons who had been born and raised in New Orleans or who had some other association with the city. The book is edited by Rosemary James, previously a reporter for WWL-TV and whom I saw on TV as early as 1967 when I started watching the news on a regular basis. She then co-founded the Faulkner society, located on Pirate's Alley in the back of the Cabildo. Her description of her first arrival in New Orleans reminded me of my own first arrival in New Orleans. And among the writers who contributed to the book were two acquaintances of mine: Mary Helen Lagasse, whom I had known since 1973 when she and I attended an English class at Tulane together. Like myself, she attended Tulane at night while working during the day. She graduated in 1978, two years after me. I knew of her writing articles for several periodicals, having read some of them. In 2004, her first novel, *The Fifth Sun,* appeared, and I read it with interest. Another contributor whom I knew but have not been in touch with is Charmaine Neville; she was one of my clients while I was a welfare worker but soon asked that I close her case, saying she had a job and could make it on her own. It was not until a long time later that I even learned that she was part of the Neville family, a family of artists.

But the back cover of the book states that it captures the city that was – and that will be again. And I fully support that cause.

By the end of October we were all back, except that most of the kids, after settling in Texas, were discharged from the Texas facility for whatever reason, and then never returned to New Orleans. But the entire staff came back. The signs of the destruction were visible all over the city. Later, in another chapter, I will discuss how the city failed to fully rebuild after the disaster.

After working the night shifts at Covenant House for a year and a half, I was suddenly transferred to the front desk because some kids had complained about my disciplinarian approaches. By that time, I already had suffered another consequence of the storm: the rent in the apartment complex in Metairie where I was so happy to live was suddenly raised to such an extent that I had to move to a cheaper apartment on Central Avenue. The apartment and the apartment complex were acceptable, however, I disliked the neighborhood, because of the crime and the drug deals that were going on in our vicinity. I saw more police patrols in that neighborhood than in any others I lived in. As for Covenant House, I had not even had time to get used to the front desk job when I was suddenly dismissed for alleged inability to do my work. I was devastated by that action, attempted to avert it, but to no avail. What frustrated me was that I had put in ten years of hard work there, even literally stuck my neck out when the storm struck; but that meant nothing to the director, the personnel director, and the rest of the administrative staff. I could not believe that I had worked for Covenant House for ten years, only to be told that there was no adequate way to employ me there. But there was nothing more I could do about that, so I turned in my identification badge and left.

ONE HAPPY YEAR

The Brotherhood of St. Andrew, of which I still was an active member, had scheduled another annual National Council meeting, this year for Washington D. C., and I had already paid for the ticket and made all the arrangements, so I went on the trip July 5, 2007. During the meeting, I shared my unfortunate experience with all participants, and all assured me of their thoughts and prayers. On July 7, a bus picked us up and drove us from Alexandria, Virginia (where the hotel was) to Washington, D.C., where we saw the White House and the several other government buildings. The bus then took us to the National Cathedral via Georgetown, which reminded me a bit of the French Quarter, and then at the cathedral, we attended an Episcopal Eucharist celebrated by one of the canons there, Eugene T. Sutton (Canon Sutton was elected and consecrated Bishop of Maryland the next year). After the Eucharist, we did some sightseeing at the cathedral, and I was fascinated by it. It is a magnificent structure and worth visiting. The next day, the meeting ended, but inasmuch as my return flight did not leave until 7:30 that evening, I took a metro tram to Arlington National Cemetery to visit the graves of John F. Kennedy and Robert F. Kennedy. I was shaking as I recited Psalm 130 and the Lord's prayer at each grave. Then I walked across the Potomac River to visit the Lincoln Memorial; again an awesome experience. I then went to Reagan National Airport and flew back to New Orleans in a plane that was one hour late in departing.

From then on, the days and weeks passed by in a routine of anxiety and frustration. After Covenant House had given me a severance pay, I spent most of my time checking the newspaper ads for jobs that I could apply for. Also, inasmuch as my termination notice did not allege any misconduct, I applied for unemployment benefits which Covenant House did not contest. (Had they done so, I would have gotten legal representation and given them a real fight.) I met with a clerk at the Louisiana Workforce Commission office to whom I described in detail what my situation was; namely, I already was 60 years old, so it would be hard to find a job. She smiled her way through my remarks and then pieced together a resume which only showed my work experience at Covenant House following receipt of my Tulane degree. In my opinion, she was totally incompetent. Of course, the resume did not help; fortunately, I had an old resume with my previous work experiences.

And after a couple of months of frustration with the job search process, I met another clerk of Louisiana Workforce while attending a church dinner, and shared my experience with him. He asked that I fax my two resumes to him at his office, and I did so the next day. Then he combined the two resumes into one and downloaded the new resumes on the computer on www.laworks.net, doing a splendid job of it. I saw the completed product on the Internet, and it was well done. Only a few days later, I received an E-mail from Donald Everard of Hope House telling me that he had seen my downloaded resume. He further informed me that Hope House had just received a grant that enabled it to engage in a homeless prevention program, and that he was considering me as a case manager with that program, with a part-time assistant also being hired. I called him, and then reported for a job interview which I felt had gone well. Then he scheduled me for a second interview for November 15, 2007, and when I reported for that interview, he told me I had the job. He then gave me all the details, and we then agreed that I should report to work Monday, November 19, 2007. After receiving the good news, I went home and called the rector (pastor) of St. Augustine's Church, Father A. J. Heine, to tell him the good news as well. He replied, "Thomas, you sound like a different man." "Of course" I replied, "now that this ordeal is over." I told a lot of my other friends about my success, and they were happy as well. Unfortunately, all my good friends had moved away from

New Orleans, both before and after the storm. In fact, the closest family that I had left were Jennie and Patrice Ann Rogers who lived in Morgan City and with whom I had spent holiday and other weekends. I also had friends in Orlando, Florida, and had already packed my books and other things in anticipation of a move, however, the day after the job opened itself for me, I unpacked everything, and made my apartment look livable again.

And then, on 19 November 2007, happy as a lark, I reported for work at Hope House. Also reporting for work that day was Joanika Davis, the part-time assistant. We had plenty of time getting acquainted and learning the routine, as the first clients did not come for help already on the first day.

The program, called Homeless Prevention, was designed to help persons in either of two situations. One situation involved persons, who because of unforeseen bills, were not able to pay their rent that month, and had received eviction notices; in that case, we reviewed their situations, ascertained that they had gotten into their situations only once, not ongoingly, and were able to be self-sufficient once we helped them. Then, we issued the rent check directly to the landlord, never to the client him/herself. Another situation involved people who were already homeless but had income and had located a place to stay; in that case, we expected that they negotiate a lease with their landlords-to-be, then apply for help, and then either Joanika or I would go out to the residence-to-be to check it for habitability. Then we would issue the check for the deposit.

Hope House is located at 916 St. Andrew Street, close to where the old St. Thomas project was. That project had been torn down and replaced by some very decent housing. Hope House was opened in 1969 and has provided several other services to the community since that time.

Donald Everard, Hope House's director, had actually been a member of the order of the Christian Brothers. I had heard others call him "Brother Don", and when I asked him about that, he told me of his Christian Brothers' experience. Therefore, hereinafter in this book, I shall refer to him as "Brother Don." He was a pleasant person to work with and for, and did a splendid job in directing Hope House in general and also in administering our program and directing the work that Joanika and I did in working it.

Sister Lilliane Flavin oftentimes impressed me as a mother-figure in directing the work that the Hope House staff did. She was a very pleasant person to deal with, and I enjoyed my dealings with her.

Janita Taylor, our receptionist, was equally pleasant to deal with, and also did a splendid job in administering the food bank at Hope House.

Catina Williams did a splendid job with Rapid Rehousing, and from time to time, Joanika's and my work crossed over with hers.

Joanika Davis, my associate in the homeless prevention program, was absolutely great to work with. I seldom enjoyed a working relationship as much as I enjoyed this one. She always had a good attitude, and also was very good at doing the financial aspect of the program, and this helped inasmuch as we had to keep close tabs on the funds we spent as we helped the families. In that aspect, she out-did me many times over. But she and I were very pleased and comfortable with each other. She, along with Janita Taylor, lived in the homes that replaced the St. Thomas Project. Every day, when she and I reported for work, we joined hands and said a prayer that God would give us the wisdom to always remember that we were serving Him as we served the needy, and do our jobs accordingly. Joanika had two twin daughters, Artesha and Artisha, and from time to time, they came to visit their mom after school, and that always made for pleasant time.

At this point, I need to share something about myself. I abhor work environments where foul language is spoken. Nor do I appreciate work places where men make sexual remarks about female employees. I believe that every work place should be decent and pleasant for all employees at all times.

The Hope House staff had weekly staff meetings every Monday afternoon after lunch. The meetings started with Brother Don recalling that we are in God's presence, and then asking for prayerful intentions from all of us. Then, after he said, "Amen", the business started, and lasted for about an hour.

The first clients started coming November 20, and Joanika and I had to get going quickly on learning the job. First, we had only people who were facing eviction. We interviewed the clients, gathered the necessary information, then prepared the cases, and showed them to Brother Don who then issued the checks to the landlords. That week was Thanksgiving Day week, and on November 21, after a full work day, I went home, packed a portable suitcase, and drove to Morgan City to spend the weekend with Jennie and Patty Ann. They also noticed my change in attitude stemming from my having another job after an anxious wait. We had a happy time together, and I returned to Jefferson on Monday after Thanksgiving to resume my work. Of course, now more than before, I realized that Thanksgiving Day is directed at God and all the goodness he gave us and is giving us in our lives.

After I returned from my Thanksgiving Day holiday, the work resumed. Joanika and I had not been given any training sessions before we started our work, so our training was totally on-the-job. Oftentimes, we consulted each other as we did our cases and completed our forms, and that's how we learned how to do the job. Brother Don, of course, gave us good directions at all times. It did not take us long to establish the procedure for helping clients through our program.

Of course, we could not help everyone. We had to observe income and rent amount limits. Additionally, we could help a family only three times, then no more.

Families had to prove to us that once they were helped, they could then make it on their own, and the standard profile form that was used for every family clearly was programmed to reflect that. Brother Don always saw to it that that requirement was complied with before he issued the checks.

Joanika and I soon got a great deal of satisfaction out of the fact that we were helping needy people. We were happy in our workplace and had a great relationship. And this meant a lot, because we had some sad situations to deal with involving unpleasant clients, landlords, and other individuals. One case I will always remember involved a young girl who took care of her wheelchair-bound father. The man had no other person to support him. Still, their landlord, without giving them adequate notice, arbitrarily evicted them from their residence, stating he needed the property for his own use. They then managed to locate one place but could not move in because the prospective landlord suddenly refused them. Finally, after a bitter struggle, they found a place for themselves. I conducted a home inspection and found the place acceptable; then Brother Don issued the check to the apartment complex where they moved in and have been living ever since.

Some homeless people did not know where to move to. Fortunately, Unity for the Homeless provided low-cost housing lists which we could give those people so that they could locate a place to stay. They then used these lists to locate such a place, negotiated leases or rental agreements with the landlords, came to us for an interview; then, after a favorable home inspection; we would issue the checks for the deposits. When a person just came for consultation, we only did a screening form, just to have a record of the contact.

The program was designed to help residents of Orleans, Jefferson, and Plaquemines parishes. However, we never received a contact from Plaquemines. At one point, a client was helped who lived on Central Avenue in Jefferson, only one block from where I was living.

Another thing that I noticed was that the rents tended to be high. My own rent was $512.00/mo, and when I looked at some other rents, I considered myself lucky. The high rents were all attributed to Katrina, repairs, and insurance costs. I personally believe that the state and local governments could have done a better job in controlling these unreasonable increases.

Our program soon became known to the community. More and more people came to us for help, and in most cases, we were able to help. The grant actually came from federal funds and was administered through the State of Louisiana Department of Social Services and Unity for the Homeless. And representatives from Unity came to Hope House from time to time to review our work, and gave us helpful hints for improvement and/or upgrading; but we were never told that we did not do our job right, and that our program should not continue. When the first inspection was done, Joanika and I quickly reviewed all our cases to make sure they were in good order, however, at inspection time, only a small percentage of cases was reviewed, and we were told we did well. Also, Hope House was not the only agency that received the grant; there were several others, and from time to time, we had to send people to these other agencies.

Joanika and I also had to take computer training, as the cases had to be entered on the computer as well. Also, we had to form a roster on a spreadsheet-type basis, and then enter each name of a person we served on the roster. Exact bookkeeping was required, as was an accurate account of the monies that we spent.

Inasmuch as our program became so well known, we were called into action after a lot of homeless people started camping out on Duncan Plaza in front of New Orleans City Hall as well as on the intersection of Canal Street and Claiborne Avenue. Joanika was able to go to these sites and talk to these dwellers, and some came to Hope House for help. When some had jobs, we were able to at least give them housing lists from Unity, and they used these lists to find a place to stay; then we helped them with the placement procedure as I described it above. Of course, in some instances, we could not help, and these people found themselves at the Ozanam Inn or the New Orleans Mission, although even these two outlets were overcrowded. After all the people who had camped out on Duncan Plaza had left, the City of New

Orleans built a fence around that plaza so as to prevent further camp-outs.

Joanika and I kept going with our work, and were happy to be part of the Hope House family. Even though the work tended to be hard at times (which is true of any social service job or any job dealing with needy people), we enjoyed doing it. At times, we had to put close tabs on some families, especially those who needed help more than once. One observation we made was that most of these families lived off minimum-wage jobs, and had a hard time making ends meet to begin with. They constantly were struggling. We encountered situations where we had to tell families to obtain low-cost housing as their rents were too high to the extent where they could not make it on the long run. But we felt that at all times, we were in the right place at the right time. And at every weekly staff meeting, we gave reports on how homeless prevention went and how successful we were, of course, with some exception. And so, for a whole year, we happily helped needy people and got a great deal of satisfaction from doing our work.

Jennie and Patrice Ann Rogers, my
two lovely Morgan City gals.

Joanika Davis and I. I seldom enjoyed a working
relationship as much as I enjoyed this one.

Artesha and Artisha Davis,
Joanika's lovely twin daughters.

Catina Williams, the manager of
the Rapid Rehousing program.

Jim Russell Records, one of
the "two pleasant neighbors."

Denise Russell and her daughter, Nicole, a perfect
mother-daughter management team.

LAGGING PROGRESS

Inasmuch as our work was taking place in Orleans and Jefferson Parishes, it was also affected by the damages caused by Hurricane Katrina, especially inside New Orleans. In fact, inasmuch as I lived in Jefferson Parish but worked in New Orleans, I could observe the difference between the two parishes whenever I crossed the parish line. I would use the Earhart Expressway to get into New Orleans, and as soon as I crossed the parish line, I could see the boarded-up houses, the water marks on some of them, and other signs of destruction that remained two years and beyond after the storm and the flood.

Of course, the storm damage was extensive. Almost 80% to 90% of New Orleans was totally flooded, and we asked ourselves if our beloved city would ever shine in its old glory. I would not be surprised to learn that public officials, such as Governor Blanco, Mayor Nagin, and others were totally overwhelmed when seeing the damage that the storm and the flooding did. My Covenant House coworkers and I kept asking ourselves what it would take to clean up New Orleans inasmuch as the flood waters were very dirty and polluted.

What occurred was that downtown New Orleans and the French Quarter were restored in that the Bourbon Street bars, the Royal Street shops, and the rest of the Quarter were restored, and they were not even flooded to begin with. Canal Street and the business district were flooded, however, as soon as possible, that district was likewise restored. The several universities and colleges throughout the city were closed for the fall semester but could reopen in the spring. I could go on and on describing other openings, but these are some examples. On a more personal note, shortly after I returned to New Orleans, I saw my doctor whose office was located across from Touro Infirmary in the Garden District. After I was finished with my appointment, I made it a point of checking the Maple Street Book Shop which I fondly remember from my college years. I drove down St. Charles Avenue until I reached Cherokee Street. There, I turned right and drove to Maple Street where I turned left and arrived at the shop. Rhoda Faust, long-time manager of the shop, saw me and made me feel that she was relieved to see me. We hugged and kissed, then shared our feelings about being relieved that we both survived the disaster. Like myself, she had also evacuated, but came back at the beginning of October to re-open the store. That store had actually been founded by her mother and aunt in 1964, as

I stated earlier. I then entered the store, and noted that it was not flooded. Had that occurred, Rhoda would have lost her whole livelihood.

Of course, a lot of others were not so lucky, and indeed lost everything. While none of my friends was killed, all of them left New Orleans, and I had no friends left. Businesses and homes throughout the city were boarded up and never reopened. And before the storm, a lot of people had evacuated; because of the extensive damage, some, whether they liked it or not, could not return, as they had neither a job not a home to go back to. I never was able to figure out the exact number of inhabitants lost in this disaster, but the loss was considerable. However, I did get to read the daily newspaper, The Times-Picayune, and it often reported on people having evacuated and then simply settled permanently in their new locations. I learned that a lot of people settled in Texas, with a large majority of these settling in Houston. At one point, I read about a family having made it all the way to Salt Lake City, Utah, and wondered how they adjusted to the climate change between the two cities. I was able to return only because Covenant House reopened; had that not occurred, I would have relocated to Orlando, Florida, where I still have some good friends.

Of course, a lot of frustration started to boil up in people's minds about the whole situation. Among the people of New Orleans, there were strong feelings about the fact that the federal government was spending money and manpower where it was not needed, such as the war in Iraq. Slogans were coined and put on bumper stickers reading, "Make levees, not war." (similar to "make love, not war" during the Vietnam war), and "Forget Iraq, Rebuild New Orleans." I fully supported these slogans. I opposed the Iraq war from the very first, and anticipated it to become another Vietnam war, which indeed it has become. George W. Bush deceived the American people into believing that Iraq was an American cause, which it never was, and started that war for no good reason.

However, as time went on, I observed more and more that the city fathers of New Orleans did not do their job properly when it came to rebuilding the city. Not enough was done to restore businesses and homes, a lot of neighborhoods remained blighted, and housing that could have helped to reduce homelessness and helped a lot of evacuated residents to return was not restored. At first, I thought that the leaders, along with everyone else, were overwhelmed by the enormity of the damage, and did not know where to start first and where to continue next, however, after a couple of months, more could have been done than was done.

While driving down the Earhart Expressway into New Orleans, I noticed that the B. W. Cooper Homes, one of the HANO-run housing projects, were fenced in for months and months, and nothing was done about restoring them so that people could move back into these homes. Later, I learned that the same was done with the remaining housing projects, except that the Iberville project, which had no damage, was re-populated. The old St. Thomas project, of course, had been razed and replaced by the current homes there which are very pleasant living places. Of course, as I already stated, these projects were not exactly ideal to live in, and I explained why. However, HANO also had scattersite homes, that is, private residences where people could live at reduced rents and had to pay utility bills as well. Additionally, there were the Section 8 residences where people lived and paid a small amount of rent, with HANO paying the bulk of the rent.

It made no sense to me that HANO and the city of New Orleans did not make a more massive effort to rebuild the projects and let evacuated residents return to them, and then make concerted plans to construct residences similar to the ones at the former St. Thomas project site. Additionally, as I later learned, there were apartment complexes in New Orleans East that also could have been restored and reopened after the destruction.

This, of course, also had an impact on our work at Hope House, because had the rebuilding been done as I described above, we could have done a better job in referring homeless people to suitable housing. Additionally, Unity for the Homeless could have had more residences available for its housing lists which it periodically updated and then made available to us.

And I often thought to myself, if New Orleans did

not do a better job in rebuilding, what would any HUD official or any other federal official think when hearing the call "Forget Iraq, Rebuild New Orleans" and then coming to the city and see this lack of local effort to rebuild? It is all right to ask for federal help in rebuilding after a disaster such as Katrina, however, the New Orleans city fathers cannot possibly and reasonably expect to get any attention, much less help, unless they make their own efforts and come up with reasonable plans to rebuild.

Shortly after our work was started, the New Orleans City Council held a meeting to decide to destroy the housing projects altogether. A lot of people were against this, including we at Hope House. In fact, several religious leaders, including Bishop Charles Jenkins of the Episcopal Diocese of Louisiana, took a stand in favor of keeping and restoring the buildings. At the city council meeting, which Brother Don attended, a scuffle erupted outside City Council chambers, and several arrests were made. Nothing could be done to prevent the destruction of these projects. Shortly there after, while passing by the B. W. Cooper Homes, I kept noticing one building after another being destroyed by the wrecking balls. And this occurred on several other project sites as well. But no new residences were built on the destroyed sites, so now there is a lot of flat land not being used for no good reason.

Another great New Orleans institution that was not renewed and reopened after Katrina was Charity Hospital, located at 1532 Tulane Avenue. That hospital dates back to 1736, and the current structure is about 80 years old. For years and years, it served at the teaching site for both Tulane and LSU medical schools which flanked that hospital for a long time. Medical students from both schools went to that hospital to do their practical training with the patients there, even after Tulane opened its own teaching hospital across the street from its medical school. A lot of students were very pleased with that learning opportunity, as it furthered their profession. Of course, the professors felt the same way. Charity also had an excellent trauma center which could be relied upon by people injured in criminal activity, such as shootings, but also due to accidents. The medical equipments at Charity also received highest commendations at all times. In every case, Charity was always there for persons who had no medical insurance so that they could get their treatment.

However, Charity Hospital was not perfect, and had its deficiencies. On that, I can share some personal experiences. In the summer of 1967, when I was having abdominal pains, my friends took me to the emergency room at Charity to have it checked. I had to wait for almost an hour before a doctor finally saw me. He told me I may have early appendicitis, then let me go. (I finally had my appendix out the following year elsewhere.) Then, in February 1975, I went to a Tulane students' function, with some faculty present, at the Tulane Alumni House. Some of my friends were there. We were seated at tables of four, and while one person spoke, one of my friends, sitting with me, suddenly passed out, and fell to the floor. The police was called, and within a few minutes, a New Orleans police officer showed up, followed by several Tulane campus police officers. They rushed my friend to Charity Hospital. Some of us, myself included, followed. When we arrived at the hospital, my friend was laying on a bed, and apparently her vital signs were checked and found to be normal. I remained with my friend, standing at her side and holding her hand. The emergency room was full of patients waiting for attention. After about an hour, a doctor finally checked out my friend for some time; then she was discharged. As it turned out, she had low blood pressure, causing the fainting spell. Still, the wait for medical attention seemed to be long.

In 1979, the mother of yet another friend of mine was taken to Charity with cirrhosis of the liver. She was placed in a large room, with about ten other patients, and I made it a point of visiting with her, along with my friend and her family. At one point, while I was visiting, another woman in the same large room, wanting attention, shook the railing of her bed real hard. I noticed that, and went to the nurses' station reporting this, and the woman was attended to.

Later that same year, I started my job as a welfare worker. One of my clients did not want any more children. She did not know that her Medicaid card covered tubal ligations, so she went to Charity to have this done. There, however, she was told that she was healthy enough to have ten more children (she already had five). She then turned to me, and was able to have her tubes tied after I checked the Medicaid manual to find that tubal ligations were indeed covered. I was furious when I learned that medical professionals would make statements of the nature that these Charity Hospital officials made, because a better informed source had told me that it is in fact not healthy for a woman to go through the birthing process over and over.

Still, despite these inadequacies, Charity Hospital was essential to the New Orleans community because of the need for treatment for uninsured persons, the need for medical students to have their practice, and the needs of victims of accidents and violent crimes resulting in injury to receive adequate medical care.

However, when Hurricane Katrina struck and devastated New Orleans, this need apparently was not recognized. The basement of the hospital was flooded, as that block of Tulane Avenue also was under water. As I stated above, the water was dirty and polluted. From my vantage point in Houston, where I went evacuating, I could tell what the disaster had done to the hospital. I learned in the media on TV that the electricity was lost, that some air conditioning was provided through a generator, but that that generator finally broke down, leaving patients and medical personnel suffocating in the heat. I also saw a picture in the HOUSTON CHRONICLE showing patients in a Charity hospital room being hardly able to stay in the hot building. After a few days, however, all patients and medical professionals were evacuated. Since then, the hospital has remained idle, with no efforts to repair and reopen it. The same fate befell the Veterans' Administration Medical Center, again a long-time facility where veterans sought their medical treatment. I know this for a fact, since my late father-in-law, Brewer F. Pence, received all his medical treatment there, having been a World War II veteran.

Because of the failure to reopen these two facilities after Katrina, uninsured patients have had to seek treatment at private hospitals at no expense, and that has in the long run caused severe financial strains on these hospitals. And we at Hope House had to help people who were not able to pay their rent because of unforeseen medical bills.

After first just hearing about it, in February 2008 I read a long article in the Times-Picayune describing a building project involving both LSU and the Veterans' Administration, by which an entire neighborhood would be torn down to build two new hospitals, one run by LSU, the other one by the VA. The article described the neighborhood, and made exaggerated comments about crime and destruction, and gave the impressions that tearing down the neighborhood and building these two hospitals would be good for New Orleans in the long run.

From the very first, when I learned of this building proposal, I thought it was utter nonsense, and I replied with a letter to the editor stating my position. When the

Times-Picayune editorialized that hospitals needed to be helped out of ICU stemming from the inability of patients to pay for their treatments, I replied with yet another letter which then was headlined, "First, fix and reopen Charity."

That neighborhood, known as Lower Mid-City, has several historic sites, and I had an interest in one of them – the Deutsches Haus, located on the corner of S. Galvez and Cleveland Streets. The building has been there since 1928; thus, it has historic significance. I had been a member there since 1998; also, since then, I have been a member of Schlaraffia, an old fun group which still meets there every Thursday. The Haus was severely damaged in the storm as well, but was fully restored since then. Today, it is still being used as a place to meet and have an enjoyable time.

I also need to recall that LSU has a very poor track record of respecting historic preservation. Decades ago, as part of its expansion, it proposed to demolish St. Joseph Catholic Church, located at 1820 Tulane Avenue.

Fortunately, a lot of people signed petitions and campaigned hard enough to the effect that the destruction project was eventually abandoned.

Because I felt all along that the proposed LSU/VA hospital project was utter nonsense and would not benefit New Orleans in any way, when I became aware of an action group that favored the restoration and reopening of Charity Hospital, I promptly joined that group. The group was, and is to this very day, very effectively chaired by Derrick Morrison and Brad Ott. And the group met several times right at Hope House. Soon, with Brother Don's consent, it placed its posters on Hope House's bulletin boards. And in meeting after meeting, it became evident that the community was suffering from the failure to reopen Charity Hospital and make it again available for needy people. We teamed up with the Foundation for Historical Louisiana, and then an architectural firm, RMJM Hillier, did an inspection of its own of the Charity Hospital building, and found it structurally sound. The firm also made several proposals to improve Charity Hospital as it was to be restored, and found that it would be more cost-effective to restore and reopen Charity Hospital that to engage in the proposed LSU/VA building project. Moreover, it was learned that it would take three years or less to restore Charity whereas it would take five or more years to build the proposed new hospitals.

Our action group met several times and went to several places, seeking support. We wrote to state legislators, city councilpersons, and other public officials. At one point, the advocates of the LSU/VA hospitals held a public forum in the auditorium at Warren Easton High School advertising their project and what good it would do. Our group, along with several others, went to the meeting. The speakers made strenuous efforts to sell their building project, then allowed members of the audience to speak. However, not one speaker from the audience favored the building of the two hospitals; all spoke against it. I was one of the last speakers, and I told the panel to just pack up the entire project, and if they were ever to hold another such meeting, I would be there again, speaking against this building project and for the reopening of Charity Hospital. After the meeting was adjourned, I walked straight up to the panel members and again made the same point. However, they did not respond, and in fact treated the entire group as is there was no good reason to oppose the building project. However, among those speaking against it were several Mid-City residents who stated that they had lived in that neighborhood for the longest, had returned after Katrina and rebuilt their homes, and simply did not want to move again. Our action group then obtained the names and addresses of these residents, and then included them among us.

It did not take too long before several other civic organizations also joined us, so we were growing as we proceeded.

The Deutsches Haus made its own efforts to save itself. I made several efforts to get them to join our action group, and even placed flyers on the premises, but had no success. In fact, the Haus placed posters reading, "The Haus and the Hospital together", under the delusion that the builders of the hospitals would respect the Haus after tearing down everything else in the neighborhood. I repeatedly spoke to members of the Haus about our action group, but did not succeed in getting them to join it. Our group, however, when dealing with the preservation of Mid-City, included the Deutsches Haus in its agenda, because I repeatedly mentioned the Deutsches Haus among the historic sites in the neighborhood.

One major historic site in that neighborhood is the Dixie Brewing Company, which had been idle for some time since it shut down. Of course, New Orleans has had this happen to two other such companies – Jax and Falstaff. Jax has been made into a shopping center, Falstaff is now an apartment complex. Dixie should also be considered for such a rebuilding effort. Personally, I had a lot of respect for the Dixie company and its contribution to the community. At one point, Dixie, while still active, used its commercial time on TV to encourage people to adopt a pet from the SPCA.

Brother Don knew of my joining the Charity Hospital action group. Additionally, he soon realized that I had agitating tendencies and used them for whatever cause I felt worthy. He was fully supportive of the Charity Hospital cause. When the action group met at Hope House in the evening, he gave me an additional key for the Hope House classroom so that I could lock it after the meeting; I then had to return the key to him the next day upon reporting to work.

Eventually, the news media started to show an interest in Charity Hospital, and what could possibly be done to the building. All along, they had reported on the LSU/VA project, which left me, for one, frustrated. However,

WWL-TV's anchorman Dennis Woltering made one attempt to see Charity Hospital from the inside, but was refused entrance. When he finally was allowed to enter the building, he noticed mold that had accumulated. Small wonder, given the fact that the rebuilding was not undertaken after the storm. I, as a member of the action group, was concerned that WWL-TV did not know about the group, so the next day I went to the station, and handed materials pertaining to our cause to Mr. Woltering himself. He told me that he was not sure if WWL-TV knew about our group, and I replied, "Well, now you know about it and have our material." Derrick Morrison and Brad Ott approved of my action when they heard about it.

I, for one, was not satisfied with just assuming that the residents of the entire neighborhood were aware of what we were doing; I wanted to know firsthand. So when Derrick and Brad decided to do a door-to-door campaign to get people to participate in rallies and make them aware of our efforts, I was happy to join. We met on the corner of Canal and South Rocheblave Streets, and divided up into two groups; one would walk down Cleveland Street, the other down Palmyra Street. I walked down Palmyra. Sure enough, we encountered several residents who did not want to leave their homes, and wanted to stay where they were. We saw a bar where a young woman told us she would lose her job if it were to close. On the corner of Palmyra and South Galvez Streets, we came across the

Sam Jupiter barber shop, and the barber told us that he had been there for a long time, and did not want to lose his business due to such a building project. I also met a man who told me he was working at Charity Hospital while it was open, and had not found suitable work after it was not reopened. And our group then gained more and more supporters who then came to our rallies.

Presently, the University Hospital, administers by LSU, has a trauma center, but that is not sufficient. Our group, at one point, held a picketing demonstration outside the Administration building on Simon Bolivar Avenue. While there, we encountered several LSU medical professors who actually supported our efforts, and told us that they felt that Charity should have been reopened a long time ago after the disaster. Among them was an old friend of mine, Dr. James Riopelle, professor of anesthesiology. Jim and I had known each other since I came to the United Stated in 1965. His father, Dr. Arthur Riopelle, and my late father, Dr. Helmut Hofer, were friends even before that time, as primatologists. Jim told me that a number of LSU medical faculty and staff supported the reopening of Charity Hospital, and that he supported our efforts.

From all data I gathered as I participated in this campaign, it appeared that the restoration of Charity Hospital would take only three years or less, whereas the proposed LSU/VA project would take five years. I firmly believe that if Charity Hospital would, if the renewal effort had been started as soon as feasible after the disaster, be an operative facility today, for the benefit of the needy people and the medical students. We would not be facing the situation that a lot of medical facilities have with uninsured patients. Of course, the Veterans Administration Medical Center should also long have been repaired and reopened. Instead, these two facilities stand idle for no good reason while political leaders, insensitive to the needs of their constituents, are debating a building project that no one would be happy with. I again raise the issue: if New Orleans talks and does not act, who wants to listen to calls for rebuilding? It makes no sense. I firmly believe that if Charity and the VA medical center had been fixed and reopened after the storm and were open now, the people of New Orleans would be better off, and the federal government would see that New Orleans had been serious about rebuilding all along, and is serious about rebuilding now.

TWO PLEASANT NEIGHBORS

I was still living in Covington in 1969 when I, after a long soul-searching job, withdrew from the Roman Catholic Church and joined the Episcopal Church. At that time, I then attended Covington's Christ Episcopal Church, however, in April 1971, I moved to New Orleans, and joined the Chapel of the Holy Spirit, located across from the Tulane University campus. Not only did I want to attend Tulane again and graduate, which I did five years later, but I also liked the University neighborhood of New Orleans. Of course, when it comes to the Episcopal Church, I knew that there are a lot of historic churches in New Orleans. One, Christ Church Cathedral, is the oldest one in New Orleans, and in all of Louisiana. Another one is Trinity Episcopal Church, which was opened in 1847, and which, along with the cathedral, has been taking the lead among all the Episcopal Churches in the Diocese of Louisiana. Trinity also has a school attached to it. And I was interested in how other churches were doing things in contrast to the chapel, so shortly after I moved to New Orleans, I attended Trinity Episcopal Church when an eminent Biblical scholar and long-time priest, The Rev. John Stone Jenkins, was instituted as rector of that church. The service was glorious, and I enjoyed every minute of it. Six years later, I again went to Trinity when a seminary dean spoke there. On that occasion, I found a very friendly atmosphere there, in that the members were close in fellowship, despite the fact that the church was quite large. Off and on since then, I maintained contact with Trinity Church. I remember William H. Barnwell, the priest who officiated at Donna's and my wedding, having joined the Trinity staff later that year, 1983. Trinity had, to my knowledge, not done very much in terms of social outreach, however, more and more, the church started engaging itself in that field.

Shortly after I started work at Hope House, I learned about a men's Bible study group that met every Wednesday morning in one of Trinity's buildings for breakfast and Bible study thereafter. Trinity Church is, of course, located on Jackson Avenue, within walking distance of Hope House, so I had an easy time first attending the breakfast and the Bible study, then driving to Hope House for work. When I joined the group, it was studying the book of Revelation, which I have difficulty in understanding in general; still, I found it interesting. John D. Wogan, a lawyer, did an excellent job in preparing notes for the study each time it met, and was an excellent coordinator.

With us for Bible study at every session was The Rev. Dagfin Magnus, a Norwegian Lutheran clergyman who served as Theologian-in-residence at Trinity. Additionally, Trinity Church had just called a new rector, The Rev. Henry Lee Hudson, who was from Alabama, graduated from Tulane University in 1974 and went to Nashotah House Seminary. After graduation and ordination, he served several churches in the rural south before being called to Trinity Church. As he later told me in a private conversation, he was happy to be back in New Orleans, and already had made several visits to the Tulane campus just so as to relive happy college memories.

The Bible study group met every Wednesday morning. The meetings started with some of the men preparing breakfast, beginning at 6:00 a.m. I always arrived between 6:00 a.m. and 6:30 a.m., and always was happy to assist in setting up the tables. John and I often arrived at the same time, and checked each other's work to make sure all forks, knives, spoons, and napkins were properly set up. Soon all the other men arrived, grace was said, then we had breakfast, after which we went to another room to study God's holy word. We adjourned at about 8:00 a.m. with a blessing by Father Dagfin, so that we all could make it to work. Although the men of Trinity Church organized the Bible study, men from other churches could join in as well. In fact, we had a Baptist clergyman amongst us who was very resourceful. As I thought of this setup, I was reminded of my activity at

St. Augustine's Episcopal Church where we had a group called "Upreach 55" which consisted of elderly members from our church as well as members of other churches. Our church provided the facility and organized the meetings, but the other members then came to them. When I shared this experience in detail with our rector, Father A. J. Heine, he told me, "That is how the larger church eventually functions", and he was right about that.

We finished studying Revelation in December 2007. then recessed for Christmas and New Year. When we resumed our study in January 2008, we decide to study the Book of Isaiah. I looked forward to that, having been familiar with passages from Isaiah as I encountered them in Haendel's "Messiah". I had become acquainted with that classical masterpiece in 1970 when singing passages from it in a church choir.

Then, in 1971, I attended a full performance of the "Messiah" at Tulane University. In January 1972, I started my job as an assistant librarian at Tulane University, and my supervisor there was a fan of classical music. When I asked him what edition of the "Messiah" he would recommend, he suggested that I get a copy of the Phillips recording, so that's what I did. That recording had all the texts in it in an accompanying booklet, and I soon realized that Haendel, when composing the "Messiah", relied heavily on the book of Isaiah in selecting the texts. Later, I attended an adult Sunday school class at a church I was visiting, and the teacher told us that Isaiah was the one prophet who most accurately predicted the life of Jesus. That was, of course, correct. So, when we started the study of Isaiah, I had a good time participating in the several classes that we held, as I had done my own study long before. And the classes were most enjoyable. Also, from time to time, as we studied the book of Isaiah, we made several references to the "Messiah", with me assisting in some of them.

As I participated in these classes and learned God's word, I also became aware of the fact that Trinity Church had a partnership with Hope House. Oftentimes, needy people would come to Trinity Church for help, and Trinity would then send them to Hope House for whatever assistance they needed. Trinity and Hope House are within walking distance of each other; from Trinity, one can walk down Jackson Avenue towards Magazine Street, then turn left towards St. Andrew Street, and then walk a block and a half toward Hope House. And, as I stated, Hope House had several services, among them a food bank. Of course, some people needed rental assistance, and we were able to help these people as well.

Brother Don and the rest of the Hope House staff noticed that every Wednesday morning, I arrived for work earlier that 9:00 a.m., the usual starting time for work. So I made him and everyone else aware of the fact that I was part of the Bible study at Trinity, and then had an easy time making it to Hope House. Additionally, they all knew of my being an active member of the Episcopal Church.

The Bible study group recessed for the summer in May. Shortly thereafter, Henry Hudson was fully instituted as rector of Trinity Church in a glorious service. I enjoyed every minute of being there. And several of the men who participated in the Bible study were there, as were clergy from other churches, including Father A. J. Heine from St. Augustine's Church. We had a splendid reception afterwards. I had left my car parked in front of Hope House, so after the reception, I went back to Hope House to get my car, and drove home.

A few weeks after that, I found an invitation to the ordination of Phoebe Roaf, a deacon at Trinity, to the priesthood. Brother Don explained to me that Trinity had sent the invitation to Hope House, and that he felt it would be appropriate for me to attend the service. Rightly so. Again, the service was beautifully done, and I enjoyed every minute of it. I had not known Phoebe before, but after the ordination, she was made associate rector of Trinity, being in effect Henry Hudson's right hand. She and I then met several times in her office after I attended the Bible study. That Bible study, after a summer break, resumed after Labor Day 2008. We finished the study of Isaiah in December of that year; the following year, we started studying small letters of the Bible from apostles other than Paul.

One habit that I have, when I have time during my

lunch hour, is to look for hangouts to spend time after eating. And all along, I had known that Magazine Street was full of antique stores where you could buy nice antiques, books etc., And I soon learned that these stores extended themselves east of Jackson Avenue towards the Irish Channel. I had seen several of them, but after a few days, one store caught my attention – Jim Russell Records. That store was opened by Jim Russell Sr. back in 1969, and I am almost embarrassed that I did not learn about it until December 2007, shortly after I had started my job at Hope House. But once I knew of the store, I made it a point of visiting it every chance I could get. At the time I became a regular customer in it, the elder Russell had already become ill and was no longer running it, so his son, Jim Jr. stood home with him. In their stead, Denise Russell, the younger Russell's wife, was running it. Later in 2008, Denise's daughter, Nicole, joined her mom in running the store after graduating from high school. The store has all its CD's in the front room, and that room also houses DVD's, VCR's, and several other disc players and CD players. Then there are two back rooms which house all records. I had not had a record player in a long time, having bought my first CD player in 1989 and then only buying CD's. Once Denise and I became acquainted, I shared with her my love for classical music, which began in 1971 with the "Messiah" and had continued since then. But I also shared with her my fascination with Olivia Newton-John, whose soft rock I liked, as well as the anti-war singers, such as Joan Baez, Bob Dylan, Peter, Paul, and Mary, and several others. I had also become acquainted with Pete Seeger, whose "Down By The Riverside" I liked. Denise and I always had a good time engaging in interesting conversations about music. From time to time, when there were sales at Jim Russell's, she would call the sales to my attention, and then I would buy a lot of CD's which I then would take to Hope House to show my co-workers before taking them home and playing them on my CD player. Also, at one point, I was able to get a free periodical at Jim Russell's which advertised a book entitled HOW CAN I KEEP FROM SINGING; THE BALLAD OF PETE SEEGER, by David King Dunaway. Denise and I also often talked about the website www.allmusic.com, which I frequently consulted on the Internet to obtain information about singers, songwriters, compositions, and anything else pertaining to music. And the Hope House staff soon knew of my being a regular customer at Jim Russell's. The store is, of course, located on the corner of Magazine and St. Mary Streets, within walking distance of Hope House. There were other stores in that neighborhood, too, but they did not catch my attention in the way Jim Russell's did. But the vicinity of the Irish Channel also reminded me of Mary Helen Lagasse and the article she wrote in MY NEW ORLEANS, the book that I had mentioned earlier. She had grown up in the Irish Channel.

HOT SUMMER ALL AROUND

One highlight of the year 2008 was, of course, the presidential election, preceded by the campaign. The candidates all started their campaigns early, and had plenty of issues to deal with. Special interest groups kept pitching in wherever they could, raising one issue after another. George W. Bush, of course, could not run for a third term, and I, for one, was glad about that. He had brought this country to the brink of disaster with his insane Iraq war. Along that line, let me point out that when the attacks of September 11, 2001, occurred, it did not take too long to figure out that Osama Ben Laden, a terrorist mastermind, was behind these attacks. Consequently, Bush was entirely correct when he demanded that the Afghan government arrest this man and turn him over to the United States, and then started the invasion of Afghanistan when the Afghans did nothing. Several other countries joined in the effort. I, for one, was fully behind President Bush, except that when a lot of Afghan suspects were flown to

Guantanamo to be imprisoned, it occurred to me that there were some innocent persons being falsely taken into custody. However, when Mr. Bush started the Iraq war, that changed things completely for me. For one thing, the Iraqi government had no relation to Ben Laden nor the September 11 attacks. Nor was there ever any proof that the weapons of mass destruction that prompted Bush to start that war even existed. I have no comment on Saddam Hussein, except that his execution did not end the Iraq war. Just like Lyndon Johnson deceived the American people into supporting the Vietnam war, with Richard Nixon continuing this deceit, Mr. Bush, portraying this cause as a great American one, deceived the people into supporting the Iraq war. To me, the parallels between these two wars were, and still are, astounding. I will make one distinction: the Vietnam war resulted in a lot of young men being drafted, whereas the Iraq war was fought by professional soldiers only. But that did little to the fact that that war also drained American manpower and also had an effect on the finances of this country. And money that could, and should, have been spent at home on domestic programs was instead spent on a senseless war. Of course, when money is spent unwisely, that has an effect on the economy. The jobless rate soared, people lost their jobs, and often their livelihoods, businesses reduced their operations or shut down completely, and the number of persons needing unemployment benefits increased at a very steady rate. This development had begun well before

2008, however, in that year, it showed its ugly face in every way.

When a man who works and supports his family faces a financial crisis, first he must stop buying luxuries, or as we call it, some of the nicer things in life, if not all of them. Then, he must cut down on necessities, such as medicines, food, clothing, and other essentials. And as he cuts on these things, his entire household suffers. It does not take long before the family cannot afford adequate health care, adequate food, and has to buy used rather than new clothes. As a result, stores selling these items simply do not make profits on them and lose revenue from sales; this in turn causes these stores to lay off their employees. Then these laid off individuals suffer, along with their families. But when no profits are made, the recession goes further and further, and as it does, it affects other enterprises, such as car manufacturers and dealers, shopping centers, and other such businesses. Ultimately, the entire economy suffers, and so do the people living under it. Apart from my work at Hope House, I became acquainted with this situation through two of my friends. First, Harriet Hyman, my realtor-friend who helped me sell the house in Chalmette, told me she was struggling to stay afloat because she had no sales of houses going on as no one could afford to buy a house. She was worried about how she was going to make it, since she still had bills to pay and keep her business going. Secondly, at one point, when I visited Denise Russell at Jim Russell's during one of my lunch hours and talked to her about this, she lamented that "people are not coming to my store to buy anything because they cannot afford it due to the bad economy." Of course, she also had to pay bills to keep up the store, and so she was struggling, too.

Another thing that plagued virtually all of us that year were the enormously rising gasoline prices, going up almost $4.00 per gallon. I, for one, had to reduce my driving to a bare bottom minimum, could not go to places I enjoyed going to, and was a virtual shut-in due to these prices.

Because Bush had dragged this country into this situation, his approval rate dropped down to an all-time low. People had fun criticizing him, and often wondered what he would do if he were caught in the economic quagmire the way the average citizen was.

Of course, I watched the campaign going on on TV as it progressed. On the Democratic side, Barack Obama and Hillary Clinton kept campaigning against each other, on the Republican side, after some campaigning, John McCain emerged as the frontrunner of his party. He, of course, deserved respect, having been a prisoner-of-war during the Vietnam war. What I cannot figure out to this very day was his support for the Iraq war, despite his own experience. I had changed my party affiliation from Republican back to Democrat after the Iraq war started. And I had voted for John Kerry in 2004. Also, I had participated in several anti-war activities; I had corresponded with United for Justice and Peace as well as CODEPINK, and had participated in two anti-war demonstrations that were held in New Orleans. So when the 2008 campaign started, I watched the campaign between Hillary Clinton and Barack Obama very closely. It was obvious that the Democrats were going to make history with either a Black man or a woman running for president. Soon, however, Barack Obama took the lead, winning one primary after another. And, of course, at convention time, he won the nomination, with the experienced Joe Biden being his running mate for Vice-President. I was familiar with Joe Biden, having seen him lecture at Tulane University in 1973 during the Direction program that year. John McCain became the Republican nominee, with Sarah Palin as his running mate.

Of course, the recession and the senselessness of the Iraq war were major issues raised. And every time I watched TV, I noticed that. I had my own TV at home, but from time to time, I was able to watch some TV at Hope House whenever the work load was not too heavy. Also, whenever I spent some of my lunch time at Jim Russell's, I was able to watch TV there, because Denise had a TV set in the front room of the store and was able to do her sales with the TV on. Denise shared my feelings about the situation, and was all pro-Obama, just like I was. Apart from her comment as above quoted, she had a lot of other critical things to say about the economic situation, because she kept feeling the pinch every day due to non-sales at her store. From time to time, I was the only person even visiting her store.

Our work at Hope House was also affected by all that, because people were not able to pay their rent due to layoffs, even after having applied for unemployment benefits. We also had people come to us for help because their work hours had been cut. And from time to time, we had to tell people to look for cheaper housing when we could not help them because they had no way of helping themselves afterwards.

At Hope House, some of us also started being politically active, and everyone supported Barack Obama for President. Campaign buttons were distributed, materials were circulated, and we all favored Obama's election. One of us, Sister Lilliane, even went so far as to pray that God would facilitate Obama's victory. Now on that, I differed. I still remembered how the so-called "Religious Right" had backed the election of Ronald Reagan as President in 1980 (I voted for Jimmy Carter in that election, and still do not feel the need to repent of that "sin", if it was a sin at all), and how Reagan, in almost pharisaic fashion, portrayed himself as God's man once he was President. His religious talk annoyed me. After he left office, that foolishness came to an end. However, George W. Bush soon revived the religious talk in an inappropriate manner. By that time, George Mitchell, just retiring as senator from Maine, had stated, "Although he is regularly asked to do so, God does not take sides in American politics."

And I never felt that God gave me any guidance whom to vote for since I became a registered voter in early 1976. He only gave me the ability to make my own decisions on this and other matters. In the 2008 election, it happened to me from time to time that friends I had in another location sent me E-mails which suggested that God was against Obama and for McCain. I consistently argued with that, pointing to Senator Mitchell's statement as above quoted. And I also gave Sister Lilliane that quotation, but she felt she had the right to stand for what she believed in. I agree, however, I would want to consider the following scenario: voter A asks God in prayer to allow McCain to win, then voter B asks God to allow Obama to win the election. How then is God supposed to decide on this? No, God stands above all differences, including political ones. And even Holy Scripture does not give us voting guidelines. So every citizen is free to decide whom to campaign and vote for, but it is wrong to drag God into a political campaign and act as if God is on the side of the candidate who is being campaigned for, and against the other candidate.

Later in this book, I will describe what I was doing on election day, November 4, 2008.

But as we at Hope House grappled with the bad economy and its effects, Joanika and I kept right on going. We kept seeing people from Monday through Thursday of each week. On Fridays, we did not see anyone, so as to be able to do all our paperwork related to our cases. Joanika did a splendid job in bookkeeping and accounting, and she and I often supported each other as we made the computer entries on each case. Since she was working part-time, there were times when she could not do the computer work, so I did it for her. But she did a splendid job in keeping me informed as to how much money was available to spend.

And that was helpful, because I myself never was good at math. My late wife always did our finances, doing a splendid job of it. She even did the income tax every year. Once she died, I was alone with these things, and that was hard. So at Hope House, I was fortunate to have Joanika with me, and that made things a lot easier for me.

Our summer schedule was reduced by half an hour each day, in that we worked only until 4:00 p.m. each day.

Hope House always shuts down for the first two weeks in August, so that its employees can take off for a vacation. And 2008 was no exception. On August 1, we disconnected and unplugged the computers and machines we had, closed all cabinets, placed all our work materials in drawers, and closed the offices altogether. Then we all left. I had planned to go to Orlando, Florida, however, when I learned that my long-time friend, John Lemon, had been sick a long time and could not have any visitors, I again went to Morgan City to spend time with my lovely relatives there, Jennie and Patrice "Patty" Ann Rogers. They and I had become close since I first visited them after Hurricane Katrina. They lived, and still live, in a house they inherited from their parents when the parents died, the mother in 1996, the father in 2004. They were struggling to make ends meet, since Jennie had not had a job for a long time, and Patty was working for minimum wage in a convenience store similar to a 7-11 or Circle K but operated inside Morgan City. Oftentimes, I have had to send them money so that they could make ends meet. But when I told them at one point that I was all alone for Thanksgiving Day, they replied, "Come and join us for Christmas", and I appreciated that as well. I had made several visits to their home, and it soon became my second home. Those two weeks, we had a happy time together watching TV, going places inside and outside Morgan City, and from time to time visiting their aunt, Helen Fremin, who lives in Bayou Vista. I now call her "aunt" myself, and have done that for along time since knowing her.

After two weeks, it was time for me to return to New Orleans and go back to work. We started our work on August 18 and soon had to deal with a lot of people who had gotten into dire straits while we were gone.

The workload was heavy, but we still were happy to help needy people. From time to time, we shared our vacation experiences, and as it turned out, everyone had a good time one way or another. And after a good vacation, returning to work was fun, too.

GUSTAV ETC.

We were back at work for two weeks after returning from vacation when our work was rudely interrupted by Hurricane Gustav as it approached New Orleans. Of course, everyone of us remembered Katrina and its devastating effects on New Orleans, so we had to brace ourselves for possible evacuation. The storm approached the Louisiana coast, and the threat became closer and closer. On August 29, 2008, three years after Katrina, the evacuation orders came out, and once again, we had to shut down everything – computers, machines, equipment – and also board up the windows at Hope House. It was the same procedure as at vacation time, with the boarding up being added. Although we realized that Gustav was not as strong as Katrina, we could not take any chances. We had to play it safe, given the effects of Katrina. And Governor Bobby Jindal, with all his faults and shortcomings, did a splendid job in issuing evacuation directives and keeping the public informed. I will give him credit for that.

Brother Don issued a memo to all of us to maintain contact with him during the evacuation period, He expressed optimism that the hurricane would bypass New Orleans and not do too much damage.

Once Hope House closed, I went home, had the oil in my car changed, then again went home to pack my two suitcases and two bags. By that time, Jennie and Patty Ann had called me and asked me to pick them up and take them with me. They had no transportation, and since the hurricane also threatened Morgan City (which was not damaged by Katrina three years earlier), I felt it was my duty to take them with me.

So on August 30, I bought batteries for my portable CD player, then finished securing my apartment, packed up whatever I needed, and drove to Morgan City. Jennie and Patty met me at their residence, and packed their belongings with mine, so soon my car was full, because they also took their dog, their hamster, and their four little birds with them. We had no definite idea where to go, and even faced the possibility of sleeping in the car. Jennie and Patty allowed me to literally call all the shots in making decisions as to where to go and how to drive. I first drove them to Opelousas, then we decided to go eastward on US-190 towards Baton Rouge. There, I turned straight into US-61 and drove northwestward until we finally located a hotel in Natchez, Mississippi. We were able to secure two rooms in that hotel, however, the management told us that we could only stay two nights and then had to leave, as all rooms were reserved from September 1 on.

Inasmuch as the drive was stressful, given the circumstances, I, for one, was glad that we had found a place at least for two nights. But I also remembered my feelings that I had after Katrina, and that had me dreary and depressed. Jennie and Patty could understand that. The day after our arrival, we went shopping at a Wal-Mart. Later that same day, I called my realtor-friend, Harriet Hyman, and she told me that she, her boyfriend, Smitty, and a friend of hers, Gerry Berggren, had made their way to Memphis, Tennessee, and when I told her that we had no place to stay after the next day, she suggested that we come to Memphis and join her there. So the next day, we checked out of the Natchez hotel and, in at times driving rain, drove US-84 eastward. I had in mind to make it to Brookhaven and check out hotels there first, but as I drove eastward, I suddenly came upon I-55 and made the instant decision to enter it and drive northward. The rain continued, making things miserable for us. We went through Jackson, then made a stop at a truck stop whose name Harriet had given me when I talked to her the day before, and had lunch there. Then, as I refilled the tank in my car, a fellow member of the Brotherhood of St. Andrew, Rudy Vartanian, called me on my cell phone, and asked me how I was faring during the storm. I told him I was evacuating, and gave him all the details on my evacuation. He told me to stay in touch with him and to feel free to call upon him should I need help with paying for any more hotels. I thanked him, and copied his number, even though I already had it on my cell phone. The we drove northward, and, after not finding any suitable hotels in Grenada, drove to Memphis. There, at the Tennessee welcome center, we were given directions to several hotels, one of which had a large bedroom where we could stay one night. The next day, I called Harriet, and she gave her phone to a Memphis friend who then directed me over the phone to a nearby IHOP restaurant. It was a strenuous drive, with me having the cell phone in one hand and the steering wheel in another; but we soon reached the restaurant, and Harriet and her company met us there. After lunch, she directed us to the hotel she and her friend were staying at. I then connected the manager of the hotel with my fellow brotherhood member who then made all the financial arrangements for the three of us to stay at the hotel. After the finances were done, the manager gave us two rooms, Jennie and Patty in one room, and me in a room right next to theirs. Once we got settled, we again visited with Harriet, and she told us that she was checking out the next day, and returning home to Slidell, as there was no damage in that city.

While in Memphis, I received a prayerful suggestion regarding hurricanes that I would like to pass on to the readers of this book. Ronald Warfuel, the President of the Brotherhood of St. Andrew, was concerned about how I was doing in the course of the evacuation, so he called me, and I told him that Rudy had agreed to finance the stay my two gals and I had in Memphis. Ron had been elected to his post at the New Orleans meeting which I had invited and hosted, and had grown a great like for me since that time. He and I agreed that we should make it an ongoing habit to pray to God to help cease these storms, and he suggested that we prayerfully remind God of the command his son Jesus gave the seas of Genesareth, "Peace, be still!"

Harriet, having been in Memphis before we came, had done some sightseeing in that city. She had visited the Memphis zoo as well as the shopping area around Beale Street in downtown Memphis. She gave us a lot of pamphlets of Memphis, among them one of Graceland Mansion, Elvis Presley's home before his death. Jennie and Patty both told me that they wanted to see a few things while in Memphis and would go crazy staying at the hotel all the time. I shared their feelings.

While in Memphis, and even while in Natchez before, we kept up with the TV reports on how the storm was going. And while we were in Memphis, the storm reached the Louisiana coast, and the eye of the storm was reported to pass straight over Morgan City. In fact, Morgan City, a little town of about 13,000 people, was prominently mentioned on the national TV stations – CNN, FOX, and the weather channel. Pictures of Morgan City were shown on television as well, and we could recognize some of the buildings and streets shown. This heightened our concerns considerably. I told Jennie and Patty that I had picked up the phrase "Forget Iraq, Rebuild New Orleans" and was about to formulate "Forget Iraq, Rebuild Morgan City." Additionally, when it came to returning from the evacuation, I was facing the possibility of not being able to return even though New Orleans was cleared for return because Morgan City had not been cleared. Day by day, we kept monitoring progress while watching television.

We found the people in Memphis to be very friendly and courteous to evacuees. And, as we watched the local news on television, we learned that there were a lot of evacuees from Louisiana in Memphis and elsewhere in Tennessee. Later, another one of my friends told me that she and her husband, who were living in Slidell, had evacuated to Chattanooga and been treated kindly there, too.

The day after we checked into the second hotel in Memphis, it rained all day long. Still, we had to do some shopping, and went to a Wal-Mart store for that. The drive was a bit long, and we were glad to make it to the store and then back again. I made it a point of keeping all my receipt for gas and meals so as to make an accurate report to FEMA upon my return. We had to eat outside all the time because the hotel had no eating facilities and no restaurant.

Inasmuch as Harriet had recommended that we visit the Memphis zoo, that's what we did the next day, September 4, 2008. Harriet had called to our attention that evacuees could receive discounts on their admission tickets to the zoo, so Jennie and Patty took their Louisiana identification cards with them, and I, of course, brought my driver's license. Among the pamphlets that Harriet had given us was a map of Memphis which showed the location of the zoo, and so I drove Jennie and Patty to McLean Road where the zoo was. We had to take two roads, and the corner to McLean Road was not clearly marked, so I accidentally drove past it. Then I stopped at a service station to ask for it. The first person I spoke to was a New Orleans woman who also had evacuated. Then an attendant gave me the correct information, so I entered that road, and drove to the zoo.

The zoo is located inside a park, and the parking space was adequate, so we had no problems leaving the car. We then entered the zoo, and the first thing we noticed was that the entrance was a courtyard consisting of two buildings built in the ancient Egyptian style. I later learned that these buildings were designed by Egyptian architects who had come to Memphis at the request of that city's administration and had the buildings constructed that way, given the fact that Memphis is named after an ancient Egyptian city. Between the buildings, there was a square with a pool in it. Of the two buildings, one housed the administration of the zoo, the other the souvenir shop.

From the very first, I noticed that the zoo was in very good sanitary condition. The animals were all well kept, and had good living spaces to dwell in. As I visited the zoo, I was reminded of the several times when my father, himself a zoologist, took my brother and me to the Vienna zoo; then, after we moved to Germany, we visited the zoo in Frankfurt several times. Both zoos were very well kept; and I made the same observation when Jennie, Patty, and I visited the Memphis zoo. I also shared that observation with the several zoo attendants that we met as we walked through the zoo. And, at the end of our visit, while Jennie and Patty browsed through the souvenir shop, I went to the administration office and again complimented the staff for the excellent condition of the zoo. After lunch, we went back to the hotel.

The next day, we visited Graceland Mansion, where Elvis Presley lived until his death in 1977. It was very interesting to see the several exhibits.

Again, as evacuees, we had a discount of the admission prices. I had wanted to see Graceland for a long time after my long-time friend, Julia F. Womack, an avid fan of Elvis Presley's, had been there herself. Of course, I had my own memories of Elvis stemming from the fact that he was stationed as a soldier in Germany for about a year and a half. He was drafted in 1958, spent basic training and another detail in the United States, then was stationed in the twin towns of Bad Nauheim/Friedberg which are located midway between Frankfurt, Germany's business capital, and Giessen, where I grew up. He completed his military service in 1960, the year I started learning English in school. The mansion was interesting to visit, as were several other sections of the whole Elvis-Presley-compound. We saw old cars that were typical of the times of Elvis Presley, then the planes he used to make his trips, and a lot of other souvenirs. There was a hotel known as Heartbreak Hotel, named after one of Elvis' songs. And we had our pictures taken at that site as well. In every case, we enjoyed ourselves, and that made a difference, given the circumstances that made us go to Memphis in the first place. When seeing the Presley family graves, I noticed a poster in German, reading, "Elvis lebt" (Elvis lives).

Throughout our stay in Memphis, we noticed the FEDEX and UPS planed flying in and out of Memphis at all times. Memphis, as we learned, has an international airport which also serves as a hub for both companies.

Every evening, we watched the progress of the possible return from the evacuation. And, after our visit to the Elvis-Presley-Compound, we again checked the news, and learned that all evacuees could safely return on September 6, the next day. So on that day, we checked out after packing our belongings, then went for a delicious breakfast at a nearby Waffle House. Then we went back home, making our way down I-55 towards the Love Truck Stop near Canton for lunch and refueling.

We spent about an hour there, because I needed to walk and use my feet and legs before they would get stiff from all that time of sitting behind the steering wheel. From there, we again drove through Jackson, bypassed

Hazlehurst, Brookhaven, and McComb while still in Mississippi, then, after crossing the state line, made a brief stop in Kentwood, bypassed Amite, entered I-12 in the vicinity of Hammond, went westward to Baton Rouge, then via I-10 to Lafayette (as we went the Baton Rouge-Lafayette stretch, we noticed cars lined up to make their way back to New Orleans), then via US-90 to Morgan City, which we reached sometime between 6:30 p.m. and 7:00 p. m. that evening. After that long drive, I, for one, was exhausted, and so spent a night with my lovely gals in their home in Morgan City, then drove back to Jefferson the next day. Fortunately, there was no flooding in Morgan City, only a lot of wind damage. New Orleans had similar damage, but nothing like the damage caused by Katrina.

That Monday, September 8, I was back at work at Hope House. After Joanika and I set up our work area again, we already received the first couple of calls for help, and soon noticed that the people had spent their rent money on evacuation expenses and, therefore, could not pay their rent. I actually was in the same situation myself, because I had to spend money that was designed for my rent; just after I returned, I received my $600.00 economic stimulus payment which helped me pay the rent. Of course, I made a FEMA claim and even went to a local FEMA office with all my receipts, however, to this date, I have not received any payments. Another thing I did was to apply for a Louisiana Purchase/food stamp card, and that I did receive, and it helped considerably with my food expenses.

We spent almost the entire month of September helping evacuees after their return. The evacuation was, of course, mandatory, and so these people had no choice. But again, we were encountering people who had low incomes to begin with, and their budgets were so lean that any unforeseen development, such as a hurricane, threw their budgets off balance. Of course, I encountered the same situation myself, and had it not been for the stimulus payment plus help I received from the church, I would indeed have been in dire straits myself.

Fortunately, New Orleans did not suffer the same damage as it did from Katrina. However, a lot of the psychological effects from the earlier storm were aggravated by Gustav. I, for one, had taken counseling for post-traumatic stress disorder due to Katrina, and needed to resume it after Gustav, because the traumatic memories kept coming back all the time. I am still living with them.

THE END THAT COULD
HAVE BEEN AVOIDED

As the month of September ended, we finally were able to help all the people who had fallen behind with their rent due to Gustav.

I myself had started to participate in an English as a second language class at church which was taught by an instructor who was a cousin of our rector and who had just moved from Memphis to New Orleans. I was there as a supply attendant, along with others. The class had actually started in September, and there were several Hispanics who were in need of learning English. I remember when I lived in Mid-City and noticed that several churches in that area had started Hispanic ministries. One such church was Grace Episcopal Church, where Donna and I were married. However, St. Anna's Episcopal Church later also started a ministry; then St. Augustine's started the class. Our students came from Honduras and Mexico.

But back to Hope House. With the effects of Gustav

being behind us, we all concentrated on the upcoming presidential election and how it would turn out. Obama, after winning the nomination of his party, soon took leads in public opinion polls; still, I for one, was not satisfied with that, and had to see him win the election. We at Hope House often talked about that; also, Denise Russell and I shared our feelings about the election as well.

But foremost on our minds was, especially Joanika's and mine, would we be able to continue our work which we liked so much? True, the grant that put us on our jobs was to expire in November, however, we were doing our job well, we received good reviews when our work was inspected by Unity for the Homeless, and so we had good reasons to believe that the proper authorities would recognize that people needed our services, and would either continue to fund the grant or get a new one. We even felt that way when we were told that we could no longer take any applications, and had to work on carefully selecting the names and numbers of people whom we could still serve, and eventually winding down the program. Joanika and I often talked about what we could do. My own campaign to save the program started on October 20, 2008. On that day, the New Orleans City Council held a budget hearing involving social services. Hope House had received a flyer announcing the hearing. After arriving for work that morning, I showed the flyer to Sister Lilliane(Brother Don was out of the office that morning), asking her if she felt I should go to that meeting and speak at it on behalf of our program. She felt that I should, so I let Joanika know where I was going, then left for City Hall. Upon arrival at City Council chambers, I completed a speaker's card, as I wanted to speak as well. Only Councilwoman Stacy Head and Councilwoman Cynthia Hedge-Morrell were at that meeting. A number of other speakers spoke, but Hedge-Morrell then asked me to speak. I went to the lectern and described our program in detail, explaining how it had helped people facing homelessness, how we helped people who had camped out in front of City Hall, how the program was threatened with termination, and that it was absolutely essential that the funds for that program be continued. Hedge-Morrell instantly agreed with me; after the meeting was adjourned, she met me at the railing, and again expressed her support for our program. I gave her one of my business cards, thanked her for her support, and agreed to keep her informed of what I, for one, would be doing. She agreed to keep in touch as well. I returned to Hope House; later, Brother Don returned in time to chair the weekly staff meeting, at which I talked at length about my experience at City Hall. We were all satisfied with the contacts I had made, but Joanika and I felt that more needed to be done to preserve the program. I wrote Hedge-Morrell a long letter again expressing my concern, but received no reply.

In response to my question, Brother Don suggested that I write to Kristy Nichols, Interim Secretary of the Department of Social Services, about continuing the grant. Additionally, he suggested that I write to the legislators in whose district Hope House is located, Senator Cheryl Gray and Representative Walt Leger III. When I suggested that I also write my representative, Cameron Henry, Brother Don agreed to my doing so. So I used our office computer, and wrote letters to all four above-named individuals. I downloaded the letters on the computer; also, I set up a folder entitled "Homeless Prevention Preservation Correspondence" and filed all copies of the letters therein. I had written all four letters on October 28, 2008, and figured to allow for reasonable time for the addressed individuals to reply.

In the meantime, election day approached. On November 3, I again went to the English as a second language class at church, and was told that the regular instructor was not available that day. The coordinator of the group then asked me to teach the class, and I agreed to do it, unprepared though I was. Still the class went well, and since I completed the material early, I then, just for the fun of it, decided to do a civics lesson. The students first learned all about the election the next day; then, after learning all about the candidates etc., a Honduran wrote the name of the president of Honduras, then a Mexican wrote the mane of the president of Mexico on the board. With that, the class closed.

The next day was, of course, election day. I got up half-an-hour early that day, and after hygiene and breakfast, drove to a fire station on Jefferson Highway to vote.

The line of voters was very long. As I waited in line, I talked to no one, as I did not want to engage and be engaged in any discussion about my choice. I happily voted for Obama, then went to work. Brother Don gave us time off at the end of the day so that we could vote, but I did not need that. From work, I went straight home that day, and turned the TV on to Channel 4, my preferred station. I had supper, and then also turned the computer on so as to keep a close watch on the election results. The polls in the Eastern states soon closed, and as the results came in, Obama soon took a resounding lead. At 8:00 p.m., the local polls closed, and the local election results also came in. At about 9:00 p.m., the presidential election returns came to a standstill. I monitored my E-mails, and was able to forward materials pertaining to the Charity Hospital reopening project. Just as I finished with that at about 10:00 p.m., I heard on TV that Obama had won the election, so I went back to the TV and saw the map of the United States, with California, Oregon ,and Washington having gone for Obama, thus placing him over the top. I remained before the TV, watched John McCain gracefully concede the election, and then, after a few local election results, watched Obama's acceptance speech in front of a huge crowd in Grant Park, Chicago. I was happy about that, and looking forward to a great future. I was also feeling for two of my friends who had supported McCain, and prepared to respect their feelings as well. But I myself had voted in elections that then went other than my vote, and had learned that that is the way the democratic process works.

The next day, I went back to work, and we were all happy about the outcome of the election. We all felt that after eight years of the miserable George W. Bush policies, a change was necessary, and the people had given a clear mandate for change with their vote. And we all looked forward to a brighter future.

Joanika and I hoped that we would be able to continue our work which we were so happy with. Even as Hope House turned away many people seeking help, we hoped that things would turn around, and even prayed for that cause. However, on November 10, we both received a memo from Brother Don which in effect told us that Homelessness Prevention, the very program that we worked for, was not being refunded, and that rapid rehousing may or may not be available. The memo added that that possibility was not even certain, nor was it certain that there would be financial support for staff. The memo ended stating that it would seem that the program would be ended as of the end of this week, which was Friday, November 14, 2008. Brother Don met with us briefly to give us copies of the memo. After he left, we both were devastated. "It looks very much like this Friday will be our last day" Joanika told me. I was so upset that I could not even talk. Although I had, amongst others, addressed Kristy Nichols about the program, I later learned that the person to address was Janice Bartley, Director, CDBG

Homeless/Housing Support. And after first being unwilling to go on further, I, having my correspondence folder in front of me, decided that before giving up, I should make follow-up contacts with the legislators I addressed as well as Cynthia Hedge-Morrell and Stacy Head. Since our workday on Monday was short anyway, I decided to make these follow-up contacts immediately after work. But before that, I went to lunch, and had only a small sandwich, as my depressed attitude decreased my appetite. After eating, I made my customary visit at Jim Russell's, and Denise could tell from my looks that something was wrong. So I told her what was going on. She wanted to know if we had considered calling in an action reporter, and I told her we had not, so she suggested that we do so, and recommended action reporter Bill Capo of station WWL-TV. After further talking, I thanked her for her suggestion and went back to Hope House. There, I told Brother Don of the suggestion I had received, and he told me he knew Bill Capo, and approved of the idea. Then, at our staff meeting, I told everyone how concerned I was that Joanika and I would become homeless due to what was about to come. Then, after the staff meeting ended, I left my car parked at Hope House, and walked to the office of Walt Leger to follow up. Although I had no appointment with him, he readily saw me, and I showed him a copy of the letter I had sent him earlier. He was quick to get into the act. In my presence, he attempted to reach Janice Bartley, but she was not in, so he left a message.

Then he told me he would write a letter to her expressing his concern about the situation, and strongly suggest that she do whatever she could to either keep the program continuing or get a new grant to renew it. I was perfectly pleased with how Leger responded to my contact, and came away with the feeling of having done something successful to keep the program going.

From Leger's office, I went to the office of Senator Cheryl Gray, located at 1100 Poydras Street. But she was not in her office, so I left a business card in her door. Then I continued my walk to City Hall to contact Cynthia Hedge-Morrell and Stacy Head. At Hedge-Morrell's office, I met her assistant, Sabrina Mays-Montana, who told me she had seen my E-mails I had sent earlier; another assistant in her office also told me that. They were all smiles, but I made it very emphatic that this was a very serious situation for a lot of people. I then succeeded in seeing Stacy Head, and she also attempted to reach Janice Bartley; again, without success. Then, after another futile attempt to see Cheryl Gray, I walked back to Hope House, told Brother Don of my contacts, and drove home.

The next day was, of course, Veteran's Day, and all government offices were closed. However, the TV stations were open, so I scheduled my contact with Bill Capo for that day, sending him an E-mail from my office computer. He replied asking for more specific data, so I sent them to him. He then E-mailed again stating he remembered how we had gotten the grant last year, and that I should tell

Brother Don that he, Capo, was interested in the grant being continued. I did that. Then, on November 12, I again E-mailed the city councilwomen as well as Rep. Leger about this. Leger faxed me a letter he had sent to Bartley, and I was very pleased with it. He laid the problem on the line for her in exactly the way I had expected, stating he knew she was aware of the homeless problem the city of New Orleans had, and how our program was helping in this situation. He concluded that he hoped that the funds could be restored so that this worthwhile program could be continued.

In response to my E-mails, Sabrina Mays-Montana e-mailed me back to say that she had left a message for Bartley to call her, and would let me know when Bartley would call back. Unfortunately, I never heard from Mays-Montana again. But I kept up my flurry of E-mails. I also called Senator Cheryl Gray, and she told me she had seen my card, and would look into the matter.

No positive results came on November 13. Then, on November 14, shortly after I arrived for work, Bill Capo called me on my cell phone to tell me he was coming to Hope House that day. He expressed a desire to speak to someone who was in need of help from us, and another client had called me to tell me she needed help, and then came to Hope House likewise. I promptly told Brother Don, and had him speak to Capo on my cell phone, too. When Capo and his cameraman arrived, I became aware that yet another woman needing help had also arrived, and she was living in the Hope House neighborhood and had just received a five-day eviction notice. She could not pay the rent because the work hours at the restaurant she was working at had been cut. Capo first interviewed her in the Hope House conference room, and she gave him a detailed description of her situation. He then turned to me, and I told him that I felt the need to help her but had no way of doing so, as we had no funds left, and I could not tell her where to get help. Then he asked me what was on my mind, and I replied, "My mind is going a million miles a minute, not even knowing what I should do first, and what I should do next, trying to stay on my feet, and stay in my place, and not being on the streets." Brother Don then added his own concerns when Capo interviewed him. As Capo and I left the conference room, he turned to me, saying, "I will be back in a couple of days, and when I get back here, I expect the grant to be back in place and you back at work here." This was most reassuring. The cameraman then filmed Brother Don and me going over some papers, then me at my desk. Joanika then escorted Capo and the cameraman to the residence of the woman needing help so that he could film it as well.

The rest of the day was dreary and somber. Joanika and I started folding up everything. She took down all the posters that we had put on the board, including one that had Gloria Steinem's signature and was mine. We placed all the folders of the people we had helped in the drawers, cleaned out our desks, and virtually dismantled our work

area. We hardly said a word to each other. Then Brother
Don gave me a nicely worded termination letter plus my
final paycheck, later also a certificate of merit signed by
all the Hope House staff. Joanika, in the course of the
clean-up, also gave me a plastic shopping bag in which
I put my beverage warmer which Jennie and Patty Ann
had given me, a picture of the two that I had hung on
my office wall, a picture cube with a few more pictures
of family and friends, and a Tulane needle plate. Joanika
and I then said a final prayer addressing the darkness of
the hour, and praying that God would see us through
it. We both felt for all the people who still needed help
so as to avoid eviction and being on the streets. And I
felt for Joanika who now had to support her lovely twin
daughters with no job. Then we both walked to the front
of Hope House, and were given farewell handshakes by
everyone. After a few words, during which I indicated that
I would continue my campaign to get the funds back, I
got into my car and drove home.

BEYOND

After I left Hope House, I drove to the bank to negotiate my final paycheck. Then I went home in thick traffic, and did not reach my residence until shortly before 6:00 p. m. I was not able to see the report that Bill Capo had made, because it aired at 5:00 p.m. while I was still on the road. However, soon after I returned home, two of my friends, including Harriet, told me they has seen me on TV. I explained all the details of the report to them. Later, as I stepped outside for a while, several more people told me about my appearance. I was a bit frustrated that they only told me they had seen me on TV without acknowledging the situation that brought about my TV appearance. After all, the report dealt with a serious situation that affected the entire community.

When I returned home, I kept the shopping bag with my belongings on my living room table as I had every intention of returning to Hope House for work and bringing the bag with me.

I had a moderate supper by myself, watched TV, checked my E-mails on my computer, and after doing a few more other things, went to bed. I did not sleep well, though.

The next day, I made my claim for unemployment benefits on the Internet. I then spent lonely hours playing CD's, watching TV, reading the newspaper for possible job ads, and spending a lonely Saturday again dealing with the ugliness of unemployment. I had been through unemployment periods before, and each was as ugly as the other.

Sunday was not different, except that I enjoyed church again, having the usual pleasant fellowship. But once I got back home, the ugliness started all over again. The Sunday paper had more job ads, and I marked off a few that I thought would suit me. In some cases, all I needed to do was to E-mail my downloaded resume. Of course, I had updated that resume so as to include my Hope House experience.

On Monday, November 17, I went to the Social Security office to reapply for my wife's benefits which I had received after losing my job at Covenant House. I had barely arrived at that office when my cell phone buzzed. It was Bill Capo calling me, and he wanted to see me that same day at my residence. I told him that I was at the Social Security office but would make it home soon thereafter. My transaction at Social Security did not take long, so I went home as quickly as I could, tidied up my living room table, and then walked in and out of my apartment, waiting for Bill Capo. He and his cameraman showed up between 11:30 a.m. and 12:00 noon, so instead of watching the noon news, I was making news again. With the camera turned on and recording me, I said, "I am unemployed and the thing about it is, I've already put in for unemployment benefits. I am going to be evicted right at the time for Christmas, and all these beautiful pieces of furniture, and the books and everything else I own are going to be thrown into the streets. I'm going to spend Christmas at the Ozanam Inn or the New Orleans Mission, and that's a hell of a thing to look forward to." As soon as I said that, the camera shut off, Capo had me sit down at my living room table, then told me, "That won't happen." He then filled me in in detail about contacts he had made, and I learned that he had contacted the Governor's office, something that Brother Don had not even suggested. He also told me that the woman who had come to Hope House with the five-day-eviction notice on Friday had been helped, and had in fact received better job offers. The two men noticed pictures and other items in my apartment, and so I did a lot of explaining. Capo at first thought I had been working for NASA Michoud when he saw a picture of it; as it turned out, that picture showed Tulane international students, myself included, as we visited that plant in November 1965. Then Capo saw a picture of Jennie, Patty Ann, and myself outside Elvis Presley's Graceland Mansion, so I explained that we were there as we had evacuated due to Hurricane Gustav. The cameraman also had me display a photo album and an old dictionary that was part of a four-volume set I inherited from my great-grandfather, August Hofer. A few more interesting things also came up, and Capo showed a genuine interest in my life and future well-being. Before he and the cameraman left, he suggested that I make it priority to look for another job, which I had decided all along. But even as he said that, he knew that I had no intention of finishing my campaign to get the grant renewed.

I will make an insertion here: when I started my campaign to renew the grant, and addressed public officials about it, I made no mention of my own situation. I figured that if I were to do that, they would reply, "Just get another job." Moreover, I have always held to the principle "God comes first, your fellow man comes second, you come third." However, Capo felt like putting my situation on the forefront, which came out in both reports, and I stood out for a number of other people who were facing a miserable plight because the grant was not renewed. That in turn made me continue bringing my situation to the attention of others, and ultimately decide to write this book. And I will admit writing a lot about myself in it.

After Capo and his cameraman left, I called Denise Russell to fill her in on what went on after her suggestion. I felt that she should know. She was sad for my job loss but happy that we had followed up on her suggestion and that things could indeed turn around. I then went to see

State Representative Cameron Henry, in whose district I was living, to talk to him about the situation as well. I had two copies of the excellent letter that Walt Leger had written to Janice Bartley, so I gave him one of them. He readily agreed that Hope House should have those funds back again so as to continue the work, and agreed that he would contact Brother Don about it, too. I then returned home and E-mailed my resume to several other agencies. I had noticed a HANO ad for some jobs, and decided to submit my resume there on Wednesday. Capo later E-mailed me that the report he did was going to be aired that Monday evening at 6:00 p.m., so I remained home until it aired. Anchorman Dennis Woltering introduced it, and first it showed the woman who had come in with then five-day eviction notice. She was elated, because after the first report aired, Hope House received several individual contributions that enabled it to help the woman with the rent.

Next came Brother Don, saying, "The number of people that are gonna be on the street are profound. We need help now, and we need serious help." Capo himself then came on the air, giving a brief account of what contacts he had made. Then came my statement as above quoted. Once the report was finished, anchorman Dennis Woltering came back on the air, saying, "Even as he searches for a new job, Thomas Hofer is continuing his campaign to get a new grant so Hope House and other non-profit agencies can help families during the economic downturn."

I found that report very well done.

The next day, as I continued sending my resume via E-mail, I received an E-mail from Councilwoman Stacy Head's office regarding a program by the Greater New Orleans Fair Housing Action Center. I had earlier received a flyer with that information, and had E-mailed my data to them, figuring that without a job, I may need their help. I acknowledged receipt of that information and stated that I would check it out further the next day.

That day, November 19, 2008, would have been the first anniversary of my work at Hope House had the grant been continued. I went to the men's Bible study at Trinity Church early in the morning. I figured that inasmuch as I was interested in returning to my job at Hope House, I should continue all my activities that I was involved in while working there. Additionally, we were still studying the book of Isaiah, and I was interested in finishing that study with all the other men. After breakfast and Bible study, I stopped by briefly to chat with Phoebe Roaf, then went to see Brother Don at Hope House to fill him in on my future plans for the grant. While at Hope House, I kept wanting the times back that I spent working there. From Hope House, I went to HANO to submit my resume for the positions that HANO was advertising. However, when I arrived at the HANO office, I could only leave my resume with the front desk clerk, and she said she would forward it to the "proper people", which I assumed were the people who would make a decision on whether or not to interview and hire me. I never heard from HANO again.

Then I went to the office of the Greater New Orleans Foundation to check out the rental assistance information I had learned about. That office was located in the Whitney Bank building on 228 St. Charles Avenue, and inasmuch as parking would have been a problem in downtown New Orleans, I parked my car in a lot in the 200 block of North Rampart Street for $4.00, then walked to the office in the Whitney building. My findings were incredible. The people at the GNO Fair Housing Center told me that they were only accepting 20 applicants out of 200 applications they had received, and were only paying $200.00 to the landlord of each applicant. Although they were not outright discourteous, I noticed that their program was grossly insufficient to meet anyone's needs and in no case an adequate replacement for the work that Hope House had been doing. I could easily have engaged them in an argument about their insufficient services, but I figured that that would only be a waste of time, so I left their office with a polite good-bye.

Given the fact that Councilwoman Stacy Head had E-mailed me with the information about that agency, I felt I needed to report to her office with my findings. So I walked up Gravier Street to Loyola Avenue which I crossed, then continued to City Hall, located on Perdido Street.

At Stacy Head's office, I saw her clerk, Ruth Idakula,

and gave her a complete account of my findings at the GNO office. I carefully described Hope House's services to her in detail, spelling out how Hope House's services were working for the community, and why GNO's services were in no way an adequate replacement for Hope House's. While Ms. Idakula and I were talking in the reception area of the City Council offices, Councilwoman Head passed by and told me she had information that the funds were actually available for the grant to continue. However, I was not able to explore this with her in detail, because she was in a hurry to get to city council chambers for another budget hearing. Idakula and I then continued talking.

My next concern was that perhaps the news media, such as WWL-TV, had received erroneous information about GNO as well. I felt I should share my information with the station, too, so I walked to that office from City Hall. At the station, I met with the receptionist and told her about my findings, adding that I wanted to leave my findings with Bill Capo in a memo. While we were still talking, anchorman Dennis Woltering came out to the reception area, recognized me, and greeted me with a friendly handshake that made me feel as if I was an old acquaintance of his. Actually, he remembered me from my television appearance two days earlier. He then wanted to know what brought me to the station, so I filled him in on what I was about to leave with Bill Capo regarding GNO. Then he decided that I could just as well speak to

Capo over the phone, and had the receptionist connect me with him. Capo at first took exception to the fact that I was engaging in activity other than a job search, but I quickly pointed out to him that I had made job contacts, including the HANO contact earlier. I also shared my GNO information with him, and as it turned out, he already knew about it. We quickly reached even keel.

From there, I went straight home, and wrote a letter to Stacy Head, sharing my concern about erroneous information being passed out that, had I not come across it and then corrected it, would have misled the public. I firmly believe that I had found out about GNO and thought that it replaced Hope House's work, however, once I realized that their program was grossly inadequate, I should raise the issue of the discrepancy I came across. I also raised the issue of the funds that she had told me in the reception area that she said were available, and asked her to specifically check into how that money could be made available to Hope House and other non-profit agencies so that they could resume their services. Stacy Head never responded to my letter and never acted on my requests.

I had rationalized all along that as a recipient of unemployment benefits, I was required to engage in an active job search. However, I also felt, and still feel, that my efforts to get a new grant for Hope House and other non-profit agencies were in every way job-search related. These days, recipients of unemployment benefits have to do everything on the computer or by phone, and do not have clerks in the Louisiana Workforce that they can talk to. Had I had someone like that available, I would have sat down with that person, explaining detail for detail how I had lost my job, and that my best bet at being re-employed was to get the grant back and be back at Hope House. I do not believe anyone would have argued with that.

My job search was an exercise in frustration. I E-mailed, faxed, wrote letters, completed applications, sent resumes, and did whatever else I could do. However, I only received calls for three interviews. The first was with a company called AFLAC. It went well, however, when the manager interviewing me told me that this was a career, not just a job, and then asked me about my age, I had to be honest with him and tell him I was 61 years old – and that was that. Next, I was interviewed by Easter Seals, and I would have gotten the job had it not been for the fact that I did not have enough college credits in sociology or social work. My third interview was with a law firm, as a file clerk. I had just completed an application at the Blood Center when a clerk in that law firm called me on my cell phone, stating she wanted to see me about a position as a file clerk, gave me the address of the firm, and had me come to the office within two hours. I arrived at the firm and had the interview, however, another person was hired, as I found out a few weeks later.

I received no further interview appointments, although I certainly went for them.

One thing that frustrated me even more so was that Catholic Charities and Odyssey House kept advertising the same jobs every Sunday but never responded after I E-mailed my resume to them. I made personal contacts at both offices, but even that produced no results. It seemed to me that if they had an opening and advertised it in the paper, then they expected to have that opening filled, and would respond to anyone answering the advertising, which is what I did every week. But that did not occur, and I cannot figure out why.

Even though a massive effort was made, I felt it was unrealistic to expect resumption of the grant by Thanksgiving, the week after Joanika and I lost our jobs. However, something could have been done to resume the grant, or get a new one, by Christmas. At least that's what I thought would have been appropriate. I had maintained contact with Brother Don and the Hope House staff, during which I also saw Joanika from time to time, so as to fill them in on my efforts. Brother Don had informed me that Representative Cameron Henry had maintained contact with him as well. Senator Cheryl Gray also contacted me at one point to tell me she was working on getting the grant reinstated. And I consulted Frances Misenheimer at Unity for the Homeless and wrote Janice Bartley myself. And the efforts that Bill Capo started were still ongoing.

However, on December 23, Walt Leger called me and told me he had spoken to Janice Bartley, and that she had told him that nothing could be done. That was, of course, devastating. However, as Leger and I continued talking, it also occurred to us that the funds for that grant came from federal funds, and that I could just as well address Senators Mary Landrieu and David Vitter as well as my congressman, Steve Scalise, about the matter. With that possibility still open, I then spent Christmas with my two lovely gals, Jennie and Patty.

One thought that crossed my mind was, and still is, how did these state officials celebrate Christmas in light of their non-action to help possibly homeless people. The scenario reminded me of the parable of the rich man faring sumptuously versus poor Lazarus on the street with the dogs licking his sores.

On January 4, 2009, I wrote letters to the two senators and to Congressman Scalise. I realized that this was the last step in my campaign to get the grant reinstated or get a new grant to resume our work. To my regret, I received no response, and so my campaign was over. I E-mailed Bill Capo with my findings, and he E-mailed me back, stating that he had no success, either. He then wanted to give me yet another interview, and we agreed to meet at my residence on January 16, 2009.

In the meantime, Jennie and Patty were facing the loss of their house, as they were not able to pay their notes on time. They knew about my loss, so they asked me to move in with them and share the expenses. I had resigned myself to not being able to go back to work at Hope House. No other agency called me about an interview. I was frustrated at having failed in my campaign to get a new grant, and figured that I could at least be useful to Jennie and Patty so that they would not be homeless.

I do not like to fail when I engage in a campaign; I like to succeed.

In preparation for the move, I engaged an old family friend, Creighton Gibson, to drive the U-Haul truck to move me. He has been a family friend on Donna's side, and he and I met January 15 to set things up.

The next day, January 16, 2009, Bill Capo and his cameraman came to my residence. Capo at first told me of the great respect he had for me and the efforts I made for the new grant, going from place to place within a short time. He then interviewed me, and I shared with him how I loved New Orleans, how I made a strenuous effort to get the new grant, and how frustrated I was at having failed in the effort. The cameraman also took a few good pictures of my residence, including one showing me participating in the opening of the Rathskeller at Tulane in 1966 and a picture of my parents and me at my graduation from Tulane in 1976. Later that day, I drove to Morgan City to be with Jennie and Patty again. Capo left a message on my cell phone to the effect that because of scheduling conflicts, the report about me would be aired later, not January 16.

Jennie, Patty, and I finalized the plans for my move, and it was set for February 14. While I visited with them, I also watched the inauguration of Barack Obama as

President of the United States. It was a glorious ceremony, and I was glad to see George W. Bush leave the office and go home to Texas. What startled me was when Chief Justice John Roberts stumbled over the words, CNN reporters had a field day making fun over the fact that the chief justice could not get 45 words right. My rationale was that from a George W. Bush appointee, you could not expect better than that.

While I was visiting with Jennie and Patty Ann, tenor Placido Domingo appeared at the Mahalia Jackson Theatre of the Performing Arts as it was being reopened after the Katrina destruction. I hated to miss that performance, as I was familiar with Domingo. He had put in joint appearances with Luciano Pavarotti and Jose Carreras, and I had bought CD's with their recordings. In 2005, he had appeared at the Gulf Coast Auditorium in Biloxi, Mississippi, and I went to see that performance. Later that same year, after the Katrina destruction, he appeared at the New Orleans arena for a performance designed to further the rebuilding of New Orleans. I went to that performance; later, I read a column by Nell Nolan, social scene columnist for the Times-Picayune, in which she commented at length about that concert, and also described how she met Placido Domingo in person. I would very much liked to have met him myself on that occasion. Because he participated in furthering the cause of rebuilding New Orleans, I have a lot of respect for him.

I returned to New Orleans the next day, and my report was aired two days later, January 23, 2009. Again, WWL-TV did a splendid job, with Bill Capo doing a splendid job in reporting. Besides myself, he also interviewed Brother Don who again did a splendid job in stating the needs that Hope House had (and I believe still has). Capo also showed copies of letters that I had written to, as he worded it, "every public officials he could think of" getting a new grant for Hope House.

Jennie, Patty, and I had agreed that I should move in with them on February 14. However, after the last report featuring primarily me aired on TV, Brother Don called me to tell me that Linda Lewis of Armstrong Family Services had called him to tell him she was interested in hiring me for a one-month-job at her agency. He directed me to call her, and so I did. The next day, I went to see her, and she hired me right away for the temporary job which was scheduled to end February 27. Linda herself had an outstanding record of community service, and Armstrong Family Services, as I learned, was named after New Orleans jazz great Louis Armstrong. Linda showed me articles about herself, of which I have one copy in which her evacuation from Katrina was described. She had planned to stay in San Joaquin County, California, but then decided to move back to New Orleans after all.

On that job, I was monitoring telephone calls for services that people needed. As I did so, I came across several people previously served by Hope House, and some of these people recognized me. Creighton and I, with Jennie's and Patty's knowledge, postponed my move to February 28.

While I was working for Armstrong, I made several farewells to New Orleans. One evening, I attended a concert at St. Louis Cathedral in which several German classical compositions were played; before that, I saw the Natchez taking off for another cruise, then had my beloved beignets at the Café du Monde. One Saturday, I went to get a haircut at the Tulane barber shop; the barber there had been at that shop when I first came to Tulane in 1965, and we exchanged memories of the times we had seen each other since after I told him of my upcoming move. After the haircut, I walked through the campus, reflecting on the good times I had there for years and years as a staff member and as a student.

At church, I had to make one farewell, too: to the Upreach 55 group that I was so happy with. I attended my last function with them on February 1, and it was hard for me to say good-bye to them.

I also had to say good-bye to the men at Trinity Episcopal Church with whom I enjoyed studying the Bible. Their fellowship had meant a lot to me as well.

At the Deutsches Haus, I had to let the Schlaraffia group know that I was leaving as well, and that was not easy for me, either, after all the good times I had spent with them.

Through the church, I had received a $1,000.00 anonymous donation, of which I was able to give Jennie and

Patty $300.00 to help them with their house note problems. They received other donations, so that eventually got them out of the hole.

My long-time Honduran friend, Julia F. Womack, and her daughter, Eslie U. Taylor, came from Slidell one day for lunch with me at Mandina's, a restaurant in Mid-City. We reflected on the good times we had in Mid-City. Julia, Eslie, and I had been neighbors until they moved to Metairie just before Donna and I got married.

Of course, I figured that once I moved to Morgan City, I could always come to New Orleans for a visit. The drive is very long, though, whatever you call 85 miles. And I had no more friends left in New Orleans, so I needed someone to stay with, as I could not afford a hotel.

The week before my move, February 21, I went to the U-Haul rental at 2801 Tulane Avenue to give my bankcard information. As I was at that place, I reflected on the time when I worked at 2601 Tulane in AFDC for ten years.

February 22 was my last Sunday at St. Augustine's, and Father A. J. said prayers with me for my well-being. I was very touched by that. After the service, a lot of people spoke to me.

Evelyn Charlton and her husband, Tom, also treated me to a farewell lunch at a New Orleans Hamburger outlet that day.

On February 23, I went back to Armstrong Family Services for my last work week, however, the restrooms were not in order, so Linda Lewis placed me on paid leave and told me to come for my final paycheck on February 27.

February 24 was Mardi Gras Day, but I spent it at home, packing, and dismantling the old closet that I inherited form my parents in 1977 when they moved back to Germany.

The next day was Ash Wednesday, and I went to church at St. Martin's Episcopal Church. I had known two deacons there, Kathleen Comer, with whom I attended school at Southeastern in Hammond from 1967 to 1969, and Priscilla Guderian Maumus, who was one of my early Tulane friends from 1965 until 1967, and whose ordination at Christ Church Cathedral December 1, 2007 I attended. However, neither one was at the service. After it was over, I went home.

The next day was my last day at the German club with Schlaraffia. I knew I could not make any more meetings after moving, because these meetings always dragged well into late night, too late for me to get back.

I had not located anyone I could stay with; actually, I am still working on that.

On Friday, just for the fun of it, I decided to visit Hope House one more time. There, I met all the good people I enjoyed working with – Brother Don, Sister Lilliane, Joanika, and a lot of others. It was pleasant to see them but sad to know that it would be along time before I could even come for a visit. I then also visited at Jim

Russell's and saw Denise. I felt bad for her, because she had made the suggestion that we engage Bill Capo in our efforts, and I so wanted to tell her that her suggestion was successful. But sure enough, I was able to buy a few more CD's. Then I went to Armstrong Family Services, picked up my final paycheck, and made my way home, finishing the packing.

Then came February 28, moving day. I got up early that day, and did a few more packing chores, especially with my clothes. Creighton and his friend showed up shortly after 8:00 a.m. had a brief breakfast, then helped me load up everything. We finished in an hour, then left. The Huey P. Long Bridge had been closed for repairs, so Creighton directed that we go Jefferson Highway to Williams Blvd. in Kenner, then turn on Airline Highway, go westward to I-310, continue till we reached US-90, and take that highway to Morgan City. We used three vehicles; Creighton drove the rented truck, his friend drove his car, and I drove my Chevy Corsica. The long drive down Jefferson Highway went well, as did the turn on Williams Blvd and the turn on Airline Highway. As I passed by the airport, I reflected on the time I had first arrived in New Orleans in 1965.

We were in Morgan City an hour and a half later. Jennie and Patty met us, and the unloading took less than an hour. Then Jennie and I escorted Creighton and his friend to the local U-Haul outlet to turn in the truck, after which Creighton and his friend left. Jennie and I then went home. She, Patty, and I had lunch, after which we did some more unpacking, and with their help, I also reassembled the old closet.

We talked and thought about how we would spend our times together. One thing we did was to take a shopping trip that took us amongst other places, to the Wal-Mart in Bayou Vista where they always did a lot of shopping. I had accompanied them several times to that store during my previous visits. And during all the visits I made with them, I often took them to see their aunt Helen, whom I now call "aunt" myself, and we talked about me taking them from time to time there again for visits. We talked about other things we would now be doing together.

In fact, their home had for a long time been a second home to me, and now it was my primary home as well. And they and I would share each other's lives from here on out. And I had to face the fact that I would now be retired, and perhaps spend a lot of time doing things that I had not done while working, such as a lot of reading, playing CD's with classical music, although I enjoy other music as well, and just generally relaxing and not having to face a time schedule.

I remember that when at one point, I went through a job interview, I was asked how long I had planned to stay in social service. I replied, "I will be a social service worker until either my death or my retirement, whichever comes first." Well, on February 28, 2009, I learned for sure that my retirement came first, as I am still alive, and will remain so until God decides otherwise. But that is in His good hands.

One of my friends had told me, "Thomas, you have spent all this time working; now enjoy yourself. Have a good time going places with your relatives, enjoy the countryside, and be happy with that." I believe that once this book is published, I will be happy. But I felt I had to write it.

After supper, and a few more friendly exchanges, we all went to bed. But before I went to sleep, I thought of the times that I would now be spending in their inherited house, and, after months and months, not even remembering the times that I had spent as a working man in New Orleans as vividly as I am remembering them now.

But on this night, I knew that my day had started in New Orleans. And I also knew that as long as I had worked, I had given it my best.